9787073027738

W0108597

THE EARLY
SCOTTISH LIMITED COMPANIES
1856-1895

THE EARLY
SCOTTISH LIMITED COMPANIES
1856-1895

An historical and analytical survey

PETER L. PAYNE
Professor of Economic History
University of Aberdeen

1980
SCOTTISH ACADEMIC PRESS
EDINBURGH

Published by
Scottish Academic Press Ltd
33 Montgomery Street, Edinburgh EH7 5JX

First published 1980
SBN 7073 0277 3

© 1980 Peter L. Payne

All rights reserved. No part of this publication may be
reproduced, stored in a retrieval system, or transmitted,
in any form or by any means, electronic, mechanical,
photocopying, recording or otherwise, without the prior
permission of Scottish Academic Press Ltd

Printed in Great Britain by
REDWOOD BURN LIMITED
Trowbridge & Esher

CONTENTS

List of Tables

List of Charts

To

Lance E. Davis

and the members of the

Division of the Humanities and Social Sciences,

California Institute of Technology

Acknowledgements

The research into the files of the dissolved Scottish Limited Companies
upon which this study is based was made possible by a grant from the
Social Science Research Council, to whom I would like to express my thanks.
The abstraction of data from the files was performed by Miss Helena
Sokolowski during 1976-77: her dedication to an extremely wearisome task
made this book possible. I am greatly indebted to her. Much of the
analysis of the data took place at the California Institute of Technology,
during my tenure as a Sherman Fairchild Distinguished Scholar for the
academic year 1977-78. For assistance in programming I would like to thank
the staff of the Willis H. Booth Computing Center, particularly Charles B.
Ray, Director of the Center, Kiku Matsumoto and Albert F. Chang. I greatly
benefited from discussion with many members of the Division of the
Humanities and Social Sciences at Caltech, particularly Lance E. Davis, J.
Morgan Kousser, Forrest D. Nelson and John Ledyard. An earlier version of
this book appeared in July 1978 as Number 222 in the series "California
Institute of Technology: Social Science Working Papers". For their critical
reading of this Paper and for numerous constructive comments, I should like
to thank my colleagues of the University of Aberdeen, particularly Alastair
Durie, Michael Fraser, Joe Kemp and Clive Lee; Rachel Britton of the
University of Essex; John Butt of the University of Strathclyde; Sir Alec
Cairncross; S.G. Checkland and A. Slaven of the University of Glasgow;
Philip Cottrell of the University of Leicester; Michael Edelstein of Queen's
College, City University of New York; the late G.H. Evans, Jr. of The Johns
Hopkins University, Baltimore, Maryland; Les Hannah of the Business History
Unit, The London School of Economics; Peter Hart of the University of
Reading; W.P. Kennedy of The London School of Economics; D.N. McCloskey of
the University of Chicago; Ranald Michie of the University of Durham, who

kindly permitted me to quote from his unpublished thesis; and W.D. Rubinstein of Deaking University, Victoria, Australia. I trust that I will be forgiven for not taking up every one of the suggestions these readers have made: I must have some omissions and errors for which to claim full responsibility! For help in both the layout and the preparation of the tables I am indebted to Mrs. Joy Hansen of Caltech. The final typescript was produced by Mrs. Pat Smith: to her and to Mrs. Lynne Bews I should like to record my gratitude. Finally, it gives me great pleasure to thank the Twenty-Seven Foundation for making a grant towards the costs of publication.

King's College
University of Aberdeen

Peter L. Payne

INTRODUCTION

Nearly half a century ago H.A. Shannon, in a seminal article, observed that "the public records of limited companies lie stacked, mile on mile, in the vaults of Somerset House, and there they have lain, some seventy years, unutilized for economic history or theory."[1] Since that time, a number of scholars have examined several facets of this source of social and economic information[2] or have dipped into it in connection with specific inquiries.[3] The files of those companies registered in Scotland, for example, have been used by Professor W. Turrentine Jackson and Dr. W.G. Kerr[4] in their studies of Scottish investment in the United States, but no British work has been done to compare with Professor G. Heberton Evans's Business Incorporations in the United States,[5] nor has any attempt been made to discover the precise magnitude or the intended purpose of the capital raised by British companies in the nineteenth century. This neglect is not entirely surprising. The volume of statistical data contained in the

1. H.A. Shannon, "The First Five Thousand Limited Companies and Their Duration", Economic History, II (1932), p.396. Shannon's other articles remain an invaluable source for economic historians. They are "The Coming of General Limited Liability", Economic History, II (1931), pp.267-291; "The Limited Companies of 1866-83", Economic History Review, IV (1932-33), pp.290-307.

2. See especially Geoffrey Todd, "Some Aspects of Joint Stock Companies, 1844-1900", Economic History Review, IV (1932-33), pp. 46-71. A more recent inquiry, as yet unpublished, is that of P. Cottrell, to whom I am indebted for some statistical material.

3. The most important study has been that of James B. Jefferys, Business Organization in Great Britain, 1856-1914, (thesis for the degree of Ph.D., University of London, 1938, and since published by the Arno Press, New York, 1978). See also his article, "The Denomination and Character of Shares, 1855-1885", Economic History Review, XVI (1946), pp.45-55.

4. W. Turrentine Jackson, The Enterprising Scot: Investors in the American West After 1873 (Edinburgh: Edinburgh University Press, 1968), W.G. Kerr, Scottish Capital and the American Credit Frontier (Austin, Texas: Texas State Historical Association, 1976).

5. G. Heberton Evans, Jr., Business Incorporations in the United States, 1800-1943 (New York: National Bureau of Economic Research, 1948).

files of the dissolved and active companies is awesome. Before the advent of the computer their analysis would have been incredibly time-consuming, if not impossible. Even with the use of a computer, the raw data still have to be collected and the sheer cost of abstracting the relevant information has inhibited systematic study of the public records of these artificial persons. This paper presents the fruits of one such inquiry. Modest as they are, it is hoped that they are sufficiently useful to stimulate further research into this potentially valuable body of materials.

It had been intended to investigate the files of the first five thousand companies registered in Edinburgh under the provisions of Joint Stock Companies Acts of 1856, 1862 and subsequent years. In the event, the grant made by the Social Science Research Council to permit the collection of data at West Register House, Edinburgh, was exhausted even before the records of the first three thousand dissolved companies had been fully examined. To have achieved so much is a remarkable tribute to the tenaciousness of my research assistant, Miss Helena Sokolowski, but the fact remains that our endeavours have been largely confined to the 2625 companies formed between 1856 and mid-1895 which had been dissolved by 1970, though it is strongly suspected that the inclusion of full data on the 311 companies formed before the mid-nineties and still in existence in 1960 would not radically have altered the nature of the results.[1]

---

1. All the files examined were of companies dissolved by 1970. The files of a number of additional companies, dissolved between 1960 and 1976, are retained by the Companies Office, Edinburgh, though stored elsewhere. It was found that the industrial distribution of companies formed before mid-1895 and still active, embodied in the statistics presented in Table 14 and Appendix 2, reflected almost exactly the distribution of the dissolved companies.

Concentration on the companies registered in Scotland has been dictated not simply by convenience and out of a desire to make a contribution to Scottish economic history but because a detailed analysis of the earliest Scottish companies permitted the coverage of a much longer chronological period than a similar investigation of an equal number of London-registered companies would have done. It must be confessed that at the outset I was almost as interested in discovering the usefulness of the computer in processing a large body of statistical data as in the data themselves. If my simple methods are found to be of value, subsequent inquiries into the public records of the limited companies - should it be felt that they are justified - can build upon and develop them.

The purpose of this paper, then, is to show how many Scottish companies were formed in each year in the second half of the nineteenth century, what they sought to achieve, how long they lived, why they passed out of existence, and just how much capital was involved. In addition, an attempt has been made to determine the magnitude of one mode of Scottish overseas investment and the possible relationship between the size, length of life and growth of the incorporated firm.

THE VITAL STATISTICS

(a) THE DATA

Some of the files of the dissolved Scottish limited companies are extremely bulky, swollen with documents, official returns, contracts, correspondence and schedules; others are thin, containing the minimum information required by statute, and a few are incomplete, their _curricula vitae_, as it were, victims of the same incompetence that contributed to their subjects' premature demise.[1] Each file is numbered in chronological order of registration and invariably contains a Memorandum of Association, signed by at least seven persons, giving the company's name, objects, nominal capital and the number of shares into which it was to be divided, and at least some of the returns which companies were required to make following their formal incorporation. Of these, the most important to this analysis is the "Summary of Capital and Shares". Made annually, this form shows _inter alia_ the number of shares taken up, the amount called up on each share and the total amount of calls received, together with the names, addresses and occupations of the shareholders. Another important set of documents within the files are copies of any resolutions to wind up the company. The manner in which these and other data have been handled may appropriately be discussed under four headings: Birth, Death and Length of Life; An Industrial Classification of the Companies; Capital and Shares; Ownership and Control.

---

1. A witness before the _Select Committee on the Companies Acts of 1862-1867_, (1877), VIII, asserted that of about 7,000 companies supposedly existing in England and Wales in 1877, as many as 5,000 had failed to make the annual returns required by the Registrar at some time or other during the previous seven years. Ques. 54-57, 87-90, 92, 213-229.

(b) BIRTH, DEATH AND LENGTH OF LIFE

Before the Companies Act of 1900 (63 and 64 Victoria, Ch.48) a
company was permitted to begin business as soon after incorporation as
its directors thought fit, however small its subscribed capital.[1] Its
date of birth is therefore clear and precise. Whatever the complications attending its conception and gestation, a company came into
being with the grant of a Certificate of Incorporation by the Registrar
of Joint Stock Companies. Fixing the date of death is much more
hazardous. For the purposes of this study, a company's duration has
been determined by the date of the winding up resolution (where a
company was wound up voluntarily) or the court order (in the case of a
company wound up compulsorily) which effectively resulted in its
subsequent dissolution, no matter how much time elapsed between this
date and the removal of the name of the company from the Register at
the Companies Office.[2] The reason for adopting this course is threefold:
the date of a winding up resolution or court order is unambiguous; the
passage of either such a resolution or order made it legally impossible
for a company to continue to carry on its business (except insofar as
might be required by the liquidator beneficially to realize and distribute

---

1. F. Gore-Browne and William Jordan, <u>A Handy Book on the Formation,
   Management and Winding Up of Joint Stock Companies</u>, 24th edition
   (London: Jordan & Sons, 1902), p.137.

2. Cf. D.H. MacGregor, "Joint Stock Companies and the Risk Factor",
   <u>Economic Journal</u>, XXXIX (1929), p.494. "The formal <u>dissolution</u> of
   these companies may be delayed for as much as a generation, as the
   public statistics show; but the winding-up order terminates their
   operating life." An extreme example among the Scottish companies
   is the Garpel Hematite Co. Ltd. (BT 2/35) which was dissolved in
   1932 under Section 295 of the Companies Act of 1929, nearly seventy
   years after the company had been ordered to be wound up by the courts
   in December 1864.

the assets); and, as it is the method adopted by Shannon, because it makes possible meaningful comparisons with English experience.[1]

Unfortunately, the lives of a large number of companies (229 or 8.7 per cent of the dissolved companies considered in this study; see Table 4 below), were not terminated by voluntary, supervisory or compulsory winding up. Some simply withered away, to be struck off the Register many years after their effective lives had ceased. To pinpoint their demise - especially if this took place before 1880 - is impossible. By the Companies Act of 1880, after a series of letters of inquiry from the Registrar to the directors or officials of such companies had gone unanswered, these firms, following an announcement in the Edinburgh Gazette, were simply dissolved.[2] As it usually took some time before the Registrar decided that a company was defunct, to use the date of gazetting in the calculation of a company's length of life tends to give an erroneous impression of longevity. A more accurate assessment of when such firms went out of business may be made by assuming that it was not long after the date of their last annual return of capital and shares. "As it is difficult to imagine why a company in effective existence should fail to

---

1. For the legal interpretation, see Gore-Browne and Jordan, op.cit., pp.341-385. Shannon's clearest statement is in "The First Five Thousand ... Companies ...", loc.cit., pp.400-401.

2. In the case of the majority of the companies being considered in this study, this took place under the provisions of Section 7 of the Companies Act of 1880. Before this Act, a company could go off the Register only by formal liquidation. Because this tended to be an expensive procedure - or, at least too expensive for an insolvent company to contemplate - many abortive and defunct companies remained on the Register despite their failure to submit the required annual returns. Although there were penalties for such default, the Registrar could not impose them unless the common informer took the initiative. See D.H. MacGregor, op.cit., pp.492-493.

make the cheap and easy returns prescribed and should ignore the Registrar's intermittent circulars on default, the assumption cannot involve any significant error."[1] Thus, unless there exists some additional evidence in the files of such delinquent companies to make greater precision possible, the date of death of companies which dissolved "in disregard of legal form" was taken as the year following the submission of their last "Summary of Capital and Shares".[2]

By following these simple but realistic rules, it was possible to determine the duration of life of the great majority of companies. Those that remain to be considered are those which cannot be said to have enjoyed any effective existence: the abortive companies. In this study, companies categorized as abortive were those (a) which lasted less than one year (i.e., from the date of incorporation to the beginning of formal winding up proceedings); (b) which made no substantive returns to the Registrar other than those necessary to qualify for a Certificate of Incorporation; (c) the contents of whose files indicated that very little or no business was conducted; and (d) whose capital was either "not subscribed for" or whose called up capital was manifestly too small to attain the stated objectives.[3]

---

1. H.A. Shannon, "The First Five Thousand ... Companies ...", loc.cit., p.401.

2. Somewhat arbitrarily, the month of the year in which it was assumed that "death" occurred was taken as that in which the first delinquent annual submission should have been made.

3. To provide just two of the many possible examples: the Bellahouston Baths Co. Ltd. (BT 2/845), dissolved under Clause 7 of the 1880 Act, was abandoned within three months of incorporation in September 1878, because "owing to bad times the Company did not float" (letter to the Registrar dated 1st November, 1879); the British and Foreign Corporation Ltd. (BT 2/1194), whose grandiose objectives included mercantile, agricultural, land mortgage and banking activities at home and overseas, was able to raise only one-tenth of its modest nominal capital of £10,000 and went into voluntary liquidation within nine months of its incorporation.

In addition to ascertaining the date of death, an attempt has been made to group companies according to the reasons for their dissolution. This information is often to be found in the wording employed in winding up resolutions, but such morbidity data are frequently as vague and misleading as contemporary medical diagnosis. Suffice it to say that, once again, Shannon's definitions have been adopted.[1] Thus, companies have been grouped (see Table 3) according to the following modes of dissolution:

1. Abortive;

2. Sold, amalgamated or reconstructed (including companies that were taken into public ownership under subsequent Nationalization Acts);

3. Wound up compulsorily, or under supervision, or by reason of liabilities - in short, insolvent;

4. Wound up voluntarily, without any reason being given, usually because the company's prospects were unfavourable or, more rarely, because the company had fulfilled the purpose for which it was started;

5. Dissolved in disregard of legal forms, or unknown, and struck off the Register under the provisions of Section 7 of the Companies Act of 1880 or the similar clauses of subsequent Acts (e.g., Section 26 of the Act of 1900; Section 295 (5), of the 1929 Act).

(c) AN INDUSTRIAL CLASSIFICATION OF THE COMPANIES

Table 14 and, in greater detail, Appendix 2, classifies the dissolved Scottish companies according to the objects for which they were incorporated. This has not been done simply by reference to the name of each company, although such titles - where they are descriptive - often furnished valuable clues to the principle purpose or purposes for which a firm came into being, and their use often tipped the balance in classifying certain cases. A

---

1. H.A. Shannon, "The Limited Companies of 1866-1883", p.293.

more important source of information was the object clauses in the Memoranda of Association, but even the use of these data presented considerable difficulty. Rarely did the subscribers to the Memoranda state the purpose of their proposed company in simple and unambiguous terms. Indeed, since a company was expressly forbidden to undertake any business not set out in its Memorandum, the law actively discouraged them from doing so. As a widely read practical guide to the formation and management of joint stock companies warned: "the greatest inconvenience follows from companies having too limited powers".[1] Accordingly, the recommendation was made that "the Memorandum should specifically enumerate all the business that the company /was/ likely to undertake".[2] In the majority of cases, therefore, it was necessary to determine the main object of a company from many that ostensibly seem to be of equal importance.

This ambiguity does not stem _solely_ from the demands of the law or the inflated claims of the promoters, but was frequently a reflection of

---

1. Gore-Browne & Jordan, op.cit., p.16. It is noteworthy that "not even the fullest sanction given by the shareholders will make valid any act which is outside the powers of the company" and undertaking such business rendered the directors personally liable for any losses sustained. A similar point was clearly made in an early number of the Accountants' Magazine: since "the expression of the objects of a company in its memorandum mainly determines what power it possesses ... it is of the utmost consequence that this part of the memorandum be so expressed as to comprehend all the powers and objects which it is anticipated the company may at any time desire to exercise .... Hence the modern practice of leaving as little as possible to implication". John Prosser, "The Incorporation of Trading Companies", Accountants' Magazine, Vol.II (1898), p.235. Italics added.

2. A number of examples were given by Gore-Browne & Jordan, op.cit., p.17: "a mining company should take power to construct railways, tramways, and canals, and not only to use them itself, but to let them out to others .... Similarly, a company which lends money on mortgage should have power to develop and turn to account or improve any land that may come into its possession".

the legitimate aspirations of the founders of the company. Conscious that success in attaining the immediate objects of their infant concerns would mean growth and diversification, the subscribers to the Articles of Association sought from the outset to avoid any subsequent legal impediment to engaging in related activities. Thus, colliery companies, for example, would seek to remove any obstacle to the mining of iron ore, iron-making, the processing of chemical by-products, the manufacture of bricks, and a miscellany of trading activities; whisky distillers anticipated the production and sale of cattle food; and land and cattle companies invariably made provision for working minerals and merchandizing either on their own account or on commission. The majority of manufacturing concerns made certain that they could "buy and sell", not only their own products but similar or related articles "brought in" from other suppliers; and banking and financial concerns cleared the way for conducting business in real estate, stocks and bonds, money-lending, and the like.

These data, coupled with the unavoidable suspicion that some promoters may deliberately have sought to disguise the true nature of their companies in order not to provoke competition or, more culpably, as a prelude to fraud, do not make for precision. Nevertheless, erroneous classifications have, it is believed, been reduced by the systematic use of supplementary information contained in the company files and by taking into account the magnitude of nominal capital, the location of the proposed company's activities and existing monographic work in Scottish economic history. Thus, a shipping company with a grandiose title and patently exaggerated objectives, possessing a nominal capital of, say, £10,000, and known from additional material in the file to have purchased a single sailing ship (or even a fractional interest in one) was classified a "single ship company" (413)[1] rather than a concern engaged in ocean shipping (411). A company called the Universal Mining and Exploration Company, whose file makes clear was engaged in tin mining in Cornwall and which operated with a called up capital of £2,500, was not placed in the "metal and coal mining and quarrying overseas" category (150) but in category 115. Several large companies apparently destined to be involved in a wide range of activities encompassing real estate, land, cattle and lumber in North America have been appropriately allocated by reference to the work of W. Turrentine Jackson and W.G. Kerr.

To provide further examples would provoke tedium. It is hoped that enough has been said to indicate that every effort has been made to achieve the maximum accuracy permitted by the available information, although doubtless errors remain. With this caveat, companies were classified according to the categories set out in Appendix 1. These are similar to those in the Standard Industrial Classification of the United States Central Statistical Board,[2] but they have been amended and supplemented to take

---

1. See Appendix 1.

2. Unites States Central Statistical Board, Standard Industrial Classification (Washington, D.C., 1939-40), Vol.I, Parts 1-4, and Vol.II, Parts 1-3. The reason why I have chosen to model my classification on the American rather than the British Classification (Central Statistical Office, Standard Industrial Classification, London: H.M.S.O., 1968), is that for my purposes the former seemed to be more convenient and because initially I had hoped to make some comparisons with the work of G. Heberton Evans, who himself employed a variant of the Central Statistical Board's classification scheme, Evans, op.cit., pp.50-53. It is perhaps necessary to emphasize that my selection of the American Classification does not invalidate any comparison with Shannon's crude categories.

account of fields of activity that were more prominent in the Scottish economy of the nineteenth century than they are today. Furthermore, an attempt has been made to distinguish between domestic and overseas enterprise in order to indicate the degree to which Scottish investment was oriented towards overseas activity. It will be observed that there are eight principle divisions, each divided into major groups. Each major group has been subdivided into a varying number of classes reflecting the activities that may usefully be distinguished in any effort to indicate the nature of early Scottish joint stock enterprise. These classes have been made as specific as the underlying information would allow. Inevitably, there is an irreducible muzziness which mirrors the behaviour of the companies themselves. To have been more precise would have been spurious; to have been less so would have reduced the present analysis to the vagueness which inhibits the use of the results of past inquiries of this kind.

(d) CAPITAL AND SHARES

Whereas Shannon, Todd and MacGregor[1] have shed much light on numerical trends in British company formation and the nature and stability of the early joint stock companies, they tell us much less about the volume of capital involved in these companies. Yet the data that would permit such a calculation are available in the annual Summaries of Capital and Shares contained in the company files. Only the enormous labour involved in their

1. See above, p.1, notes 1-3; p.5, note 2. Earlier studies of joint stock companies, based on the Parliamentary returns, were made by Leone Levi. They are to be found in the Journal of the Royal Statistical Society, XXXIII (1870), pp.1-41, and XLIX (1886), pp.214-264.

abstraction and, in a pre-computer age, their manipulation can explain
this neglect. Even for this analysis of the first three thousand Scottish
companies the task has been extremely time-consuming.[1] Three basic
magnitudes are involved: the nominal capital, the called-up capital and the
denomination of shares.[2] All of these, in the case of each company, could
change over time. The nominal capital, initially specified in the
Memorandum of Association, usually remained unaltered for several years
after incorporation. Indeed, the size of original "capital" was typically
pitched so high that this figure often served most companies throughout
the entire span of their existence, but a thriving company invariably
increased its nominal capital with the passage of years. Conversely,
after 1877, less successful concerns, particularly those adversely
affected by periodic bouts of depression and those anticipating voluntary

---

1. As a consequence, it has also been expensive compared with the
traditional inspirational and intuitive methods which often provided
"guesstimates" of remarkable accuracy but whose reliability was
always suspect. It may be worth emphasizing that the opportunity
cost of the quantitative approach can be very high but it is an
inevitable and necessary price to be paid if economic and social
historians are to make further progress in a wide variety of inquiries.
The point is well expressed by my colleague, C.H. Lee, in his elegant
essay The Quantitative Approach to Economic History (London: Martin
Robertson, 1977), p.98.

2. Jefferys, "The Denomination and Character of Shares ...", using the
Limited Liability Joint Stock Companies List, Burdett's Official
Intelligence, Parliamentary Papers and a wide variety of sources,
including company prospectuses and investment circulars and manuals,
provides, as always, the best introduction to this subject.

liquidation, tended to write down their capitals.[1] The share denominations of the great majority of companies, established at birth,[2] tended to remain inviolate. This is not to say that changes could not be made - the subdivision of shares of large amount into shares of smaller amount was permitted by the Companies Act of 1867 - but, with the exception of overseas mortgage, land and cattle companies, they appear to have been comparatively infrequent among the Scottish companies in the period under consideration.[3]

---

1. The rules governing alterations in capital are clearly set out by Gore-Browne & Jordan, op.cit., pp.311-29. Whereas, unless specifically forbidden by its Memorandum or Articles of Association, a company could increase its capital by the passage of either an ordinary or special resolution, the reduction of capital, until expressly allowed by the Companies Act of 1877, required the sanction of the Courts. Even after the Act of 1877, a reduction of capital was attended by numerous procedural complications. Not surprisingly, as Essex-Crosby has observed, "reduction of capital was not a dominant feature in company affairs before the /First World/ War. From 1894 onwards the average number of yearly cases rose from 13 in the period 1894-95 ... to an average of 28 before 1908-1911". A. Essex-Crosby, Joint-Stock Companies in Great Britain, 1890-1930 (University of London: unpublished M.Comm. thesis, 1937), pp.150-51. If the Scottish data are any guide, I suspect the number of British cases was somewhat higher than this between 1877 and 1890. Certainly, the procedure was employed after the collapse of the ranching craze in the mid-'eighties by many cattle and land companies and, at home, for example, Donnachie provides details of two cases of the reduction of capital in brewing (Meiklejohn & Sons of Alloa, in 1893, and D.S. Ireland Ltd. in 1896). Ian Donnachie, A History of the Brewing Industry in Scotland (Edinburgh: John Donald, 1979), pp.170-71.

2. The importance attached to the denomination of shares in a company has been emphasized by Jefferys, "The Denomination ... of Shares", pp.45-55. "Probably no point ought to be more anxiously weighed", wrote an adviser to limited companies in the 'sixties, 'than the nominal amount of the shares into which the capital of the company is to be divided'", Loftus Fitz-Wygram, Limited Liability Made Practical. Reduction of the Capital of Companies and the Sub-Division of Shares (London, 1867), quoted Jefferys, ibid., p.45.

3. The issue of shares of a different (and, invariably lower) denomination than those by which companies established themselves was fairly common. In the compilation of Table 13, the convention has been used of employing that denomination of share by which, at any one time, the majority of the capital was raised.

In comparison with the nominal capitals and the share denominations, the statistics relating to the amount of capital called up (sometimes referred to as the issuedor paid-up capital) are extremely volatile, even effervescent. Rarely a year went by without changes in these figures. It must be assumed that it is this characteristic which has hitherto discouraged attempts to calculate the magnitude of the paid-up capital of British joint stock companies at different periods of time. For this analysis, note was taken of every change in the total amount of calls received by every dissolved Scottish company formed between 1856 and mid-1895 up to and including 1914. This information was entered on punch cards, but to reduce the vast number of cards that complete coverage would have necessitated, the conventions were employed that marginal additions or subtractions made to the called-up capital (involving changes of less than 2 per cent) were either ignored or averaged and that within these limitations the maximum possible accuracy was to be achieved for December in each year. Even then nearly 9,000 cards were required. The foregoing discussion may be clarified by the tabulation of two illustrative examples (Table 1).

(e) OWNERSHIP AND CONTROL

Since the statutes governing the establishment and conduct of joint stock companies required _inter alia_ the annual submission to the Registrar of lists of shareholders[1] and of any changes that took place among the

---

1. The lists had to show the names, addresses, occupations and share holdings of each member of the company.

TABLE 1

TWO ILLUSTRATIONS OF CHANGES IN CAPITAL AND SHARES

(a) Burntisland Oil Co. Ltd. (Incorporated, 5 September 1881; Dissolved, 8 September 1892. Industrial Classification: 326)

Date	Nominal Capital (£s)	Share Denomination (£s)	Capital Called Up (£s)
December 1881	120,000	10.00	61,460
January 1883	120,000	10.00	103,450
December 1885	140,000	10.00	119,450
December 1887	170,000	10.00	144,950
February 1892	170,000	10.00	169,470

(b) Prairie Cattle Co. Ltd. (Incorporated, 30 December 1880; Dissolved, 1 March 1915. Industrial Classification: 914)

Date	Nominal Capital (£s)	Share Denomination (£s)	Capital Called Up (£s)
December 1881	200,000	10.00	50,000
December 1882	200,000	10.00	62,500
December 1883	500,000	10.00	212,212
December 1884	500,000	10.00	250,000
December 1885	600,000	10.00	284,901
December 1888	600,000	10.00	294,055
December 1889	600,000	10.00	378,755
December 1890	600,000	10.00	421,649
December 1892	300,000	5.00	176,930
December 1894	300,000	5.00	205,814
December 1895	300,000	5.00	222,229
December 1899	165,000	2.75	102,919
December 1900	225,000	2.75	135,419
December 1901	165,000	2.75	152,919
December 1903	235,000	1.75	180,855
December 1904	235,000	1.75	190,000
December 1913	235,000	1.75	227,470

Source: SRO, Dissolved Companies Register, BT2/1049A (Burntisland Oil Co.) and BT2/1003 (Prairie Cattle Co.).

directorate - the first directors being named in the original Articles
of Association[1] - the company files contain a mass of material relating
to the ownership and control of the incorporated companies. Although
these data have not been entirely ignored - much information relating to
these matters was collected during the examination of the files - their
potential value has not been exploited in this study. To have done so
would have involved prodigious labour and postponed almost indefinitely
the appearance of this exploratory essay.[2] All the various sampling
methods considered possessed grave drawbacks. Fearsome statistical
difficulties were encountered in any inquiry going beyond the simple
counting of heads, and even this relatively simple calculation obscured
what appeared to be a widening dispersion of share-ownership which was
itself of kaleidoscopic variety. At the present stage of computer
technology, it would seem - given realistic cost constraints - that
valid generalizations concerning the ownership and control of British

---

1. It is possibly helpful to mention that the Memorandum of Association
   was the Charter of the company, while the Articles of Association,
   which governed the company's internal affairs, may be thought of as
   its by-laws. Unlike the Memorandum, the Articles of Association might
   from time to time be altered by the members without the intervention
   of the Court, and to an almost unlimited extent. Gore-Brown & Jordan,
   op.cit., p.39; see also Prosser, op.cit., p.234.

2. The point was made in a letter to the author by Sir Alec Cairncross
   that "what nobody seems to have done is to study Scottish wills so as
   to see what sort of portfolio the wealthier Scots held". Such an
   investigation is now underway by Dr. W.P. Kennedy and Rachel Britton
   as part of an S.S.R.C.-sponsored research project: "Aspects of British
   Foreign Investment, 1865-1939" (Ref: HR 4963). I am indebted to Miss
   Britton for letting me see her preliminary papers: "Sampling Scottish
   Inventories, 1876-1915" and "Private Investors in the U.K., 1870-1913".
   On the basis of the evidence of the probate records, Rubinstein has
   shown the great wealth amassed by several nineteenth century Scottish
   businessmen. Among those leaving over £2 million were Sir Charles
   Tennant, Peter Coats, Sir James Coats and William Weir. W.D.
   Rubinstein, "The Victorian Middle Classes: Wealth, Occupation, and
   Geography", Economic History Review, 2nd Series, XXX (1977), pp.602-
   23.

companies implicit in their files must remain a tantalizing prospect, and
that currently these data may most fruitfully be used in enquiries limited
to particular years, specific industries, small groups of companies and
even individual businesses.

II

THE DEMOGRAPHY OF THE EARLY SCOTTISH
JOINT STOCK COMPANIES

Nearly 3000 companies were incorporated in Scotland between 1856
and mid-1895 (2936), or about 6 per cent of all companies formed in the
United Kingdom during this period (Table 2). Of these, 311 were still
in existence in 1960; 2625 had been dissolved (Table 3).

The annual number of companies formed in the United Kingdom and
in Scotland before the First World War is presented in Chart I. The
periodicity will be immediately apparent. The correspondence between
peaks and troughs of company formation and the trade cycle is equally
clear when the turning points of the latter[1] are superimposed upon the
curves (see Chart I). Crude though the annual data are, they suggest
that peaks in company formation occurred at or shortly before the upper
turning points of the general cycle. Similarly, years characterized by
relatively low company formation, tended to be those at or near
(generally preceding) the lower turning points. The evidence suggests a
high degree of correlation between movements in incorporation and general

---

1. To indicate the peaks and troughs of the general business cycle, I
   have employed the calendar-year reference dates tabulated by Arthur
   F. Burns and W.C. Mitchell, Measuring Business Cycles (New York:
   National Bureau of Economic Research, 1946), p.79.

TABLE 2

NUMBER OF COMPANIES REGISTERED UNDER THE COMPANIES ACTS: SCOTLAND AND UNITED KINGDOM, 1856-1914

Year	(1) Scotland	(2) United Kingdom	(1)/(2) %	Year	(1) Scotland	(2) United Kingdom	(1)/(2) %
1856	8	230	3.5	1886	93	1,891	4.9
1857	23	393	5.9	1887	97	2,050	4.7
1858	14	306	4.6	1888	125	2,550	4.9
1859	6	331	1.8	1889	137	2,788	4.9
1860	15	416	3.6	1890	148	2,789	5.3
1861	24	483	5.0	1891	157	2,686	5.8
1862	34	512	6.6	1892	164	2,607	6.3
1863	31	790	3.9	1893	189	2,617	7.2
1864	27	997	2.7	1894	207	2,970	7.0
1865	38	1,034	3.7	1895	261	3,892	6.7
1866	38	762	5.0	1896	308	4,735	6.5
1867	18	479	3.8	1897	332	5,229	6.3
1868	25	461	5.4	1898	392	5,182	7.6
1869	19	475	4.0	1899	333	4,975	6.7
1870	19	595	3.2	1900	340	4,966	6.8
1871	48	821	5.8	1901	211	3,433	6.1
1872	85	1,116	7.6	1902	254	3,929	6.5
1873	63	1,234	5.1	1903	264	4,075	6.5
1874	66	1,241	5.3	1904	247	3,831	6.4
1875	48	1,172	4.1	1905	290	4,358	6.7
1876	69	1,066	6.5	1906	329	4,840	6.8
1877	88	990	8.9	1907	337	5,265	6.4
1878	64	886	7.2	1908	272	5,024	5.4
1879	65	1,034	6.3	1909	414	6,373	6.5
1880	70	1,302	5.4	1910	353	7,184	4.9
1881	76	1,581	4.8	1911	353	6,444	5.5
1882	114	1,632	7.0	1912	401	7,367	5.4
1883	117	1,766	6.6	1913	409	7,425	5.5
1884	113	1,541	7.3	1914	384	6,214	6.2
1885	78	1,482	5.3				
				TOTAL	9304	154,817	6.0

SOURCES: Col.1: 1856-1894, Appendix Table 2; 1895-1914, The Stock Exchange Official Intelligence, Vol.XI (1922), p.1790.
Col.2: 1856-1862, Shannon, "The First Five Thousand ...", p.421; 1863-1914, The Stock Exchange Official Intelligence, Vol.XI (1922), p.1790.

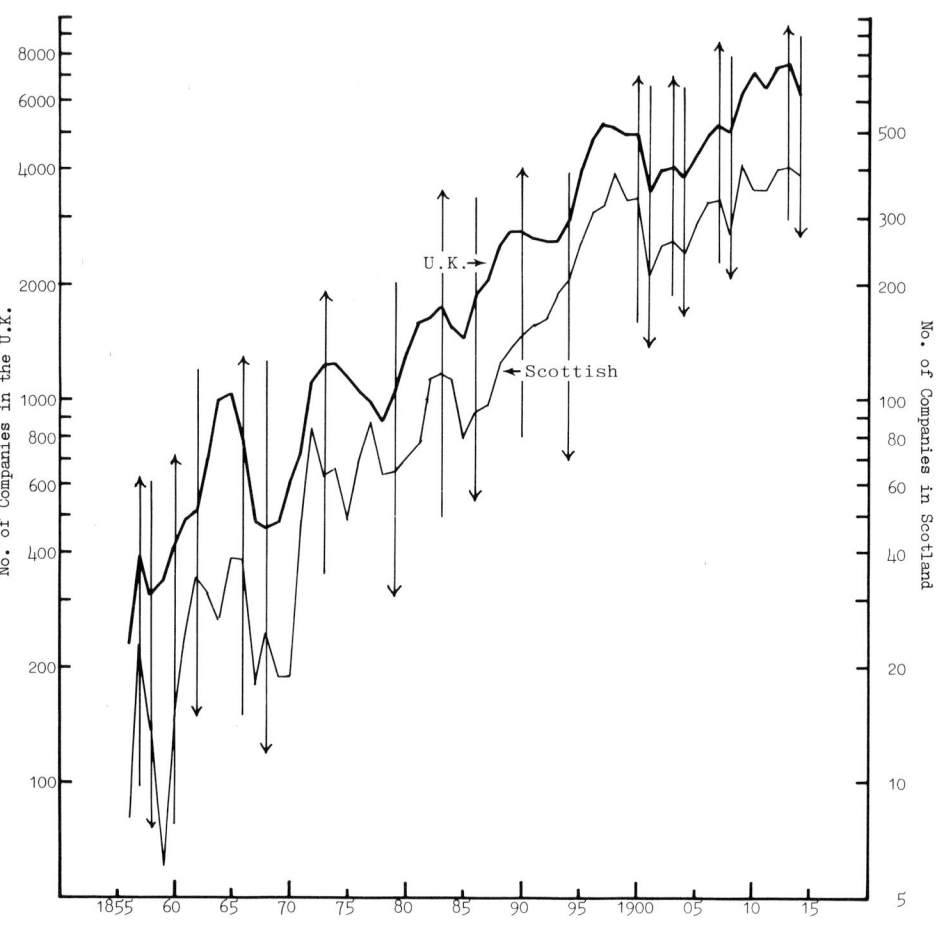

CHART 1:   Companies Formed, 1856-1914

TABLE 3

ANNUAL DISSOLUTIONS OF SCOTTISH COMPANIES (INCLUDING ABORTIVES) INCORPORATED
BETWEEN 1856 AND MID-1895 BY MAJOR INDUSTRIAL GROUPS

Year	100 Mining & Quarrying	200-300 Manufacturing	400 Public Utilities	500-600 Trade	700 Service	800 Finance, Insurance, & Real Estate	900 Agriculture, Forestry, & Fishing	Total
1856	–	–	–	–	–	–	–	–
1857	–	–	–	–	–	–	–	–
1858	–	2	4	–	–	1	–	8
1859	–	–	–	1	1	1	–	1
1860	1	2	1	–	–	–	–	3
1861	1	2	1	–	–	–	2	5
1862	2	1	2	–	–	–	1	6
1863	3	3	4	1	1	3	1	10
1864	3	1	3	1	1	4	1	15
1865	4	1	6	1	1	2	1	10
1866	–	3	1	1	2	2	1	12
1867	1	5	2	1	1	1	2	13
1868	3	6	5	–	–	1	1	12
1869	1	2	4	1	–	1	2	16
1870	1	1	8	2	–	–	2	6
1871	3	2	4	1	–	1	1	9
1872	6	6	6	1	–	1	1	18
1873	5	3	2	1	–	–	–	13
1874	7	5	5	1	3	3	3	21
1875	3	5	7	2	3	3	4	29
1876	5	11	10	3	3	7	3	27
1877	8	13	13	4	4	3	4	47
1878	7	7	7	1	4	3	3	40
1879	6	8	10	1	5	7	1	40
1880	4	10	8	1	4	5	1	35
1881	4	7	6	1	3	5	3	31
1882	9	14	6	3	6	12	1	39
1883	5	12	15	3	5	10	3	59
1884	7	16	4	1	9	9	4	44
1885	5	16	14	–	4	6	6	46
1886	4	16	12	3	10	6	2	56
1887	7	15	12	5	9	7	5	57
1888	4	22	14	6	3	12	4	61
1889	7	17	14	2	9	15	3	64
1890	7	21	12	5	8	4	2	59
1891	10	23	13	4	3	12	2	67
1892	9	30	16	2	6	7	1	72
1893	8	31	22	3	6	5	5	76
1894	10	33	17	3	10	14	3	89
1895	10	28	17	2	8	16	3	84

Year	100 Mining & Quarrying	200-300 Manufacturing	400 Public Utilities	500-600 Trade	700 Service	800 Finance, Insurance, & Real Estate	900 Agriculture, Forestry, & Fishing	Total
1896	17	36	18	6	7	8	7	99
1897	6	24	24	2	8	4	5	73
1898	12	28	21	4	7	13	4	89
1899	9	27	18	4	3	3	7	71
1900	3	25	14	1	5	6	3	56
1901	5	13	18	4	7	6	2	55
1902	9	14	13	3	5	6	3	52
1903	5	11	13	1	5	3	1	37
1904	4	15	11	4	4	9	2	47
1905	3	6	11	1	8	3	1	31
1906	2	7	10	–	6	5	2	31
1907	4	10	13	1	4	5	2	39
1908	2	10	12	1	2	9	3	39
1909	3	5	13	–	6	3	2	31
1910	–	6	17	2	3	1	1	27
1911	1	5	9	2	1	2	1	21
1912	2	5	7	1	2	2	3	21
1913	2	2	5	1	2	1	1	12
1914	5	6	11	1	2	2	2	27
1915	1	1	3	–	1	1	1	10
1916	1	6	8	1	2	2	1	14
1917	1	5	15	–	1	1	1	25
1918	1	5	6	–	2	1	1	15
1919	–	2	13	–	2	2	2	19
1920	1	6	13	1	7	4	2	27
1921	–	4	6	1	5	1	–	16
1922	2	8	4	3	1	2	1	18
1923	–	3	5	–	5	5	1	17
1924	1	5	4	1	4	1	1	18
1925	–	3	4	–	1	–	1	11
1926	1	4	6	1	1	1	1	11
1927	–	2	–	1	1	1	1	5
1928	–	4	1	1	1	–	1	7
1929	–	1	1	1	2	1	1	4
1930	–	4	1	–	1	1	1	7
1931-40	3	34	18	3	8	7	1	74
1941-50	6	10	45	4	14	7	1	87
1951-60	12	11	9	1	12	13	2	60
1961-70	–	10	5	–	4	8	1	27
1856-1975	**291**	**773**	**704**	**116**	**284**	**331**	**126**	**2625**

business activity and tends to confirm the findings of Alfred Marshall and D.H. Macgregor.[1] G.H. Evans, following a more rigorous analysis of a much larger American population, came to the same conclusions. He observed: "one might almost have been led to predict that peaks in incorporation would follow peaks in business. Promoters, however, seem to sense the approach of a recession, or at least grow wary, and curtail incorporating activities while prosperity still has a high degree of momentum. Their bearishness doubtless contributes toward bringing on a recession. On the other hand, their preparations for a revival precede an upturn and most certainly contribute to the spirit of optimism that characterizes expansions".[2]

It is arguable that a good indicator of business confidence is the nominal capital of the companies formed in each year. Movements in this annual figure perhaps constitute a barometer of economic optimism equally as sensitive as the simple number of companies incorporated. The total nominal capital of (dissolved) Scottish companies formed in each year between 1856 and 1895 is presented in Table 17. Ignoring the first few years (when the magnitudes are relatively small), peaks and troughs in total nominal capital, like those in company formation, have a tendency to precede the turning points in the trade cycle.

There is no such close correspondence between dissolutions and the general movements of the economy. It might have been expected that a graph of company deaths would produce something like a mirror image of

1. Alfred Marshall, Industry and Trade (London: Macmillan, 1919), p.334; D.H. Macgregor, Enterprise, Purpose and Profit (Oxford: Oxford University Press, 1934), pp.81-6.

2. G.H. Evans, op.cit., p.88.

births, attaining peaks at times of depression and troughs during periods
of prosperity. That this did not occur in the case of the Scottish
companies may perhaps be explained in terms of a complex combination of
entrepreneurial expectations, the self-interest of company directors,
and legal factors. It has been observed elsewhere[1] that despite perpetual
public ululations concerning the state of trade, the majority of nineteenth
century business men clung steadfastly to the hope, even belief, that
"things would get better". It took a relatively long period of unprofit-
able activity before they reluctantly became convinced that their
companies had little prospect of future prosperity. Indeed, in the case
of limited companies, several, if not the majority of, individual members
of boards of directors had little incentive voluntarily to go into
liquidation. The leading spirits on the board, among whom, for example,
might have been the inventor whose patent was to be exploited by·the company
or the original proprietor or partners of the firm whose business formed
the nucleus of the joint-stock company, stood to lose nearly everything
by a premature winding up; whereas, as Marshall put it, if they allowed
"the speculation to run on, any additional loss /would/ fall on /the/
creditors; and any gain /would/ come to /themselves/".[2] Moreover, with
reserves of capital subscribed and unpaid,[3] nearly all limited companies
possessed a greater buoyancy than unincorporated firms, permitting them

---

1. P.L. Payne, Rubber and Railways in the Nineteenth Century (Liverpool:
   Liverpool University Press, 1961), pp.159-60.

2. Alfred Marshall, Principles of Economics, 8th edition, (London:
   Macmillan, 1920), p.590.

3. See below, p.46.

to stay afloat at least until the body of shareholders refused to answer additional calls and preferred to forfeit their shares rather than throw good money after bad. All this, coupled with a desire to postpone the relatively heavy costs of winding up, meant that distressed companies possessing any freedom of action tenaciously held on, so that when they were forced into liquidation not only did they have large and ruinous liabilities[1] but the unfavourable business conditions which had contributed to their terminal illnesses had frequently given way to a cyclical upturn.

Since nearly half (46 per cent) of the early Scottish companies formed between 1856 and 1895 that had been dissolved by 1970 were wound up voluntarily (see Table 4) and an additional 9 per cent (Mode of Dissolution Type 5) simply withered away, it is hardly surprising that there is but little coincidence between the pattern of total dissolution and the trade cycle. The very term "voluntary liquidation" implies the possession by the board of at least some latitude in timing the initiation of winding up proceedings. Firms wound up compulsorily had no such powers of manoeuvre. The courts could wind up any company unable to pay its debts,[2] a process usually initiated in the case of the companies examined in this paper by a petition presented by one or more of its creditors. Taking only those Scottish companies wound up compulsorily

---

1. A fact emphasized in B.P.P., 1877, VIII (419), Ques.2197-8, 2454-5, 2468-70.

2. It is almost unnecessary to mention that this somewhat bald statement hardly does justice to the legal niceties involved in the determination of when a company is deemed to be unable to pay its debts or when the Court will order a compulsory winding up. The subject is discussed by Gore-Browne & Jordan, op.cit., pp.341-8.

TABLE 4

YEAR AND MODE OF DISSOLUTION OF SCOTTISH JOINT STOCK COMPANIES INCORPORATED BETWEEN 1856 AND MID-1895 AND DISSOLVED BEFORE 1970

Mode of Dissolution (a) / Year	(1) Abortive Number	%	(2) Sold, Amalgamated or Reconstructed Number	%	(3) Insolvent Number	%	(4) Voluntary Liquidation Number	%	(5) Struck off Register Number	%	Total Number	%
1856	-	-	-	-	-	-	-	-	-	-	-	-
1857	-	-	-	-	-	-	-	-	-	-	-	-
1858	1	12.5	-	-	1	12.5	5	62.5	1	12.5	8	0.3
1859	-	-	-	-	1	100.0	-	-	-	-	1	0.0
1860	1	33.3	-	-	-	-	1	33.3	1	33.3	3	0.1
1861	2	40.0	-	-	-	-	3	60.0	-	-	5	0.2
1862	3	50.0	-	-	-	-	2	33.3	1	16.7	6	0.2
1863	2	20.0	-	-	2	20.0	5	50.0	1	10.0	10	0.4
1864	7	46.7	1	6.7	1	6.7	5	33.3	1	6.7	15	0.6
1865	5	50.0	-	-	-	-	3	30.0	2	20.0	10	0.4
1866	4	33.3	2	16.7	-	-	6	50.0	-	-	12	0.5
1867	2	15.4	-	-	1	7.7	4	30.8	6	46.2	13	0.5
1868	-	-	2	16.7	1	8.3	9	75.0	-	-	12	0.5
1869	2	12.5	-	-	2	12.5	10	62.5	2	12.5	16	0.6
1870	-	-	1	16.7	-	-	4	66.7	1	16.7	6	0.2
1871	4	44.4	1	11.1	-	-	4	44.4	-	-	9	0.3
1872	6	33.3	-	-	1	5.6	10	55.6	1	5.6	18	0.7
1873	5	38.5	1	7.7	2	15.4	4	30.8	1	7.7	13	0.5
1874	9	42.9	1	4.8	1	4.8	10	47.6	-	-	21	0.8
1875	3	10.3	6	20.7	5	17.2	14	48.3	1	3.4	29	1.1
1876	5	18.5	4	14.8	3	11.1	13	48.1	2	7.4	27	1.0
1877	9	19.1	11	23.4	4	8.5	20	42.6	3	6.4	47	1.8
1878	8	20.0	3	7.5	6	15.0	18	45.0	5	12.5	40	1.5
1879	9	22.5	2	5.0	11	27.5	11	27.5	7	17.5	40	1.5
1880	4	11.4	8	22.9	10	28.6	7	20.0	6	17.1	35	1.3
1881	4	12.9	3	9.7	14	45.2	7	22.6	3	9.7	31	1.2
1882	9	23.1	8	20.5	10	25.6	9	23.1	3	7.7	39	1.5
1883	9	15.3	11	18.6	14	23.7	14	23.7	6	10.2	59	2.3
1884	9	20.5	7	15.9	13	29.5	14	31.8	1	2.3	44	1.7
1885	5	10.9	7	15.2	12	26.1	15	32.6	7	15.2	46	1.8
1886	10	17.9	9	16.1	19	33.9	15	26.8	3	5.4	56	2.1
1887	7	12.3	5	8.8	10	17.5	28	49.1	7	12.3	57	2.2
1888	7	14.8	8	13.1	17	27.9	24	39.3	3	4.9	61	2.3
1889	8	12.5	10	15.6	18	28.1	18	28.1	10	15.6	64	2.4
1890	3	5.1	15	25.4	13	22.0	25	42.4	3	5.1	59	2.3
1891	5	7.5	13	19.4	18	26.9	21	31.4	10	14.9	67	2.6
1892	9	12.5	8	11.1	23	31.9	30	41.7	2	2.8	72	2.7
1893	11	14.5	6	7.9	28	36.8	27	35.5	4	5.3	76	2.9
1894	15	16.9	5	5.6	27	30.3	35	39.3	7	7.9	89	3.4
1895	8	9.5	10	11.9	17	20.2	43	51.2	6	7.1	84	3.2
1896	1	1.0	29	29.3	11	11.1	49	49.5	9	9.1	99	3.8
1897	-	-	15	20.5	16	21.9	36	49.3	6	8.2	73	2.8
1898	1	1.1	24	27.0	10	11.2	55	49.4	10	11.2	89	3.4
1899	-	-	23	32.4	10	14.1	32	45.1	6	8.5	71	2.7
1900	1	1.8	13	23.2	7	12.5	30	53.6	5	8.9	56	2.1
1901	-	-	10	18.2	11	20.0	26	47.3	8	14.5	55	2.1
1902	-	-	5	9.6	7	13.5	32	61.5	8	15.4	52	2.0
1903	-	-	7	18.9	10	27.0	18	48.6	2	5.4	37	1.4
1904	-	-	10	21.3	8	17.0	25	53.2	4	8.5	47	1.8
1905	-	-	3	9.7	6	19.4	19	61.3	3	9.7	31	1.2
1906	-	-	6	19.4	5	16.1	19	61.3	1	3.2	31	1.1
1907	-	-	9	23.1	10	25.6	20	51.3	-	-	39	1.5
1908	-	-	3	7.7	15	38.5	12	30.8	9	23.1	39	1.5
1909	-	-	10	32.3	5	16.1	12	38.7	4	12.9	31	1.2
1910	-	-	2	7.4	4	14.8	19	70.4	2	7.4	27	1.0
1911	-	-	3	14.3	2	9.5	14	66.7	2	9.5	21	0.8
1912	-	-	1	4.8	1	4.8	14	66.7	4	19.0	21	0.8
1913	-	-	3	25.0	1	8.3	8	66.7	-	-	12	0.5
1914	-	-	7	25.9	6	22.2	11	40.7	3	11.1	27	1.0
1915	-	-	1	10.0	-	-	8	80.0	1	10.0	10	0.4
1916	-	-	1	7.1	1	7.1	11	78.6	1	7.1	14	0.5
1917	-	-	5	20.0	-	-	19	76.0	1	4.0	25	1.0
1918	-	-	2	13.3	2	13.3	10	66.7	1	6.7	15	0.6
1919	-	-	4	21.1	1	5.3	12	63.2	2	10.5	19	0.7
1920	-	-	4	11.4	4	11.4	23	85.2	-	-	27	1.0
1921	-	-	3	18.8	3	18.8	9	56.3	1	6.3	16	0.6
1922	-	-	5	27.8	-	-	13	72.2	-	-	18	0.7
1923	-	-	4	23.5	4	23.5	9	52.9	-	-	17	0.6
1924	-	-	1	5.6	2	11.1	13	72.2	2	11.1	18	0.7
1925	-	-	2	33.3	-	-	4	66.7	-	-	6	0.2
1926	-	-	4	36.4	3	27.3	4	36.4	-	-	11	0.4
1927	-	-	2	40.0	2	40.0	1	20.0	-	-	5	0.2
1928	-	-	-	-	3	42.9	3	42.9	1	14.3	7	0.3
1929	-	-	1	25.0	-	-	2	50.0	1	25.0	4	0.2
1930	-	-	1	14.3	1	14.3	5	71.4	-	-	7	0.3
1931-1940	-	-	18	24.3	19	25.7	34	45.9	3	4.0	74	2.8
1941-1950	-	-	46 (b)	52.9	4	4.6	34	39.1	3	3.4	87	3.3
1951-1960	-	-	8	13.1	7	11.5	38	64.0	7	11.7	60	2.3
1961-1970	-	-	8	29.6	1	3.7	15	55.6	3	11.1	27	1.0
1856-1970	215	8.2	471	17.9	504	19.2	1206	46.0	229	8.7	2625	100.0

Notes: (a) The Modes of Dissolution are more fully explained in the text, p.8, the information given in the column headings provides only a guide.

(b) Includes 29 Gas Companies nationalized under the Gas Act, 1948, and the Gas Vesting Date Order, 1949.

(Table 3, Mode of Dissolution Type 3), there is a clear inverse relationship between the number of companies dissolved by this method and the general course of business (Chart 2).

It is equally apparent that there is a marked positive correlation between the course of the trade cycle and movements in the series of those companies sold, amalgamated or reconstructed (Mode of Dissolution Type 2). Clearly, it was easier to sell out and, conversely, to raise the capital necessary to buy out or effect an amalgamation during periods of prosperity. Where the data are available, it is apparent that a substantial number of the Scottish companies that were sold as "going concerns", particularly those concerned with overseas ventures, were taken over not by firms registered in Edinburgh but by English companies, and that the locus of power was transferred from Glasgow, Edinburgh or Dundee to somewhere south of the border, usually London.[1]

It remains to consider the abortive companies. The 215 companies which can so be described (Table 5) are distributed throughout the period 1856-1895 without any apparent relationship with the trade cycle. The implication is that there were more factors affecting successful birth than those that can be loosely described as "financial". Doubtless, the state of the money market was influential in determining the ability to float a company, but equally important, it might be supposed, were the plausibility of the company's objectives, the degree of competition already existing in its proposed field, and the reputations and known abilities of the signatories to its Memorandum and Articles of Association. There were

---

1. The genesis of this movement, which dates from the 1850's, has been examined by David S. Macmillan, "The Transfer of Company Control from Scotland to London in the Nineteenth Century: The Case of the Scottish Australian Company, 1853", Business History, XII (1970), pp.102-115.

No. of
Cases

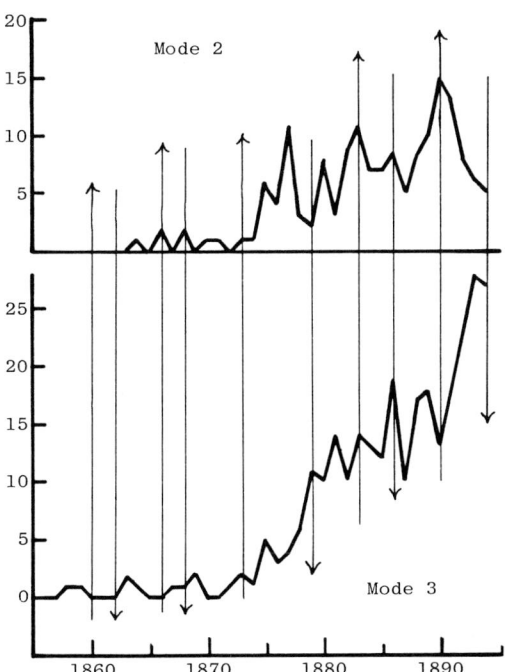

CHART 2: Annual Dissolutions of Scottish
Companies by Mode 2 and Mode 3, 1856-1894

TABLE 5

AN INDUSTRIAL CLASSIFICATION OF (ABORTIVE) SCOTTISH JOINT COMPANIES FORMED
BETWEEN 1856 AND 1895, BY MAJOR INDUSTRIAL GROUPS

Year	100 Mining & Quarrying	200–300 Manufacturing	400 Public Utilities	500–600 Trade	700 Service	800 Finance, Insurance, & Real Estate	900 Agriculture, Forestry, & Fishing	Total
1856	-	-	-	-	-	-	-	-
1857	-	-	-	-	-	-	-	-
1858	-	1	-	-	-	-	-	1
1859	-	-	-	-	-	-	-	-
1860	-	-	1	-	-	-	-	1
1861	1	1	1	-	-	-	-	3
1862	1	-	3	-	-	-	-	4
1863	-	-	1	-	-	-	-	1
1864	-	-	4	-	1	1	-	6
1865	-	-	1	-	-	3	1	5
1866	1	2	-	1	-	-	-	4
1867	-	1	-	1	-	-	-	2
1868	-	-	1	-	-	-	-	1
1869	-	-	1	-	-	-	-	1
1870	-	-	-	-	-	-	-	-
1871	-	1	2	1	1	-	-	5
1872	2	3	3	1	1	-	-	10
1873	3	-	2	-	-	-	-	5
1874	1	3	2	-	1	3	-	10
1875	1	-	-	-	-	-	-	1
1876	-	2	-	1	-	1	-	4
1877	-	2	2	2	-	2	-	8
1878	-	2	2	-	2	2	-	8
1879	-	3	3	-	1	2	-	9
1880	-	-	2	1	2	2	-	7
1881	-	1	-	-	-	3	-	4
1882	-	3	1	-	3	3	-	10
1883	1	4	2	1	2	1	1	12
1884	-	2	1	-	2	2	-	7
1885	-	5	1	-	1	-	-	7
1886	2	-	1	-	3	1	-	7
1887	-	2	2	1	-	-	-	5
1888	-	1	1	2	1	3	1	9
1889	1	3	-	-	1	3	1	9
1890	-	2	-	-	-	-	-	2
1891	-	2	-	2	-	1	-	5
1892	1	8	-	1	1	-	-	11
1893	-	4	4	-	1	3	-	12
1894	1	4	-	1	3	4	-	13
1895	1	3	1	-	1	-	-	6
Total*	17(1)	65(1)	45(2)	16(3)	28(6)	40(9)	4(2)	215(24)
Proportion(%)	7.9	30.2	20.9	7.4	13.0	18.6	1.9	100.0(11.2)

* Figures in brackets show the number of companies primarily or solely
intended to engage in overseas enterprise.

too a number of random factors: the failure to discover mineral wealth where exploratory surveys initially suggested favourable prospects; the sudden death of the leading promoter; the shipwreck and total loss of a vessel expected to fulfil the hopes of the members of a single-ship company. One thing is noteworthy. Only 7 per cent of the Scottish companies formed in the period up to mid-1895 were abortive. This is much less than the comparable figure for companies registered in London. Shannon talks of over 1,200, constituting (with a number of "small" companies) no less than 36 per cent of the total London registrations in the decade 1856-1865;[1] nearly two thousand, or 31 per cent of registrations during 1866-1874; and 3,311, or 35 per cent, for the period 1875-1883. "We may say", he commented, "that in the first quarter-century or so of limited liability the investor rejected more or less out of hand about one-third of the proposals submitted to him."[2] Even in the 'eighties, MacGregor found that about a quarter of all companies were abortive.[3]

Some part of the difference between the London and Edinburgh registrations is undoubtedly due to the tighter definition of abortiveness adopted in this essay. For example, it is probable that some of Shannon's abortive companies (which are nowhere properly defined) would under my definition be deemed effectively formed, albeit to enjoy only a short life on a small called up capital. But this can be only a partial explanation,

---

1. Shannon, "The First Five Thousand ...", p.402. Shannon distinguishes 220 "small" companies, with an average paid-up capital of under £300, only 50 of which lasted for more than three years.

2. Shannon, "The Limited Companies of 1866-1883", pp.292-93. Todd, op.cit., p.55, assumes 35 per cent of the early London registrations to be abortive; Levi (J.R.S.S., XXXIII, 1870) produced a similar estimate for the 1860's.

3. Macgregor, "Joint Stock Companies ...", pp.496-97. He calculated that 30 per cent and 27 per cent of all the London companies registered in the decades 1893-1902 and 1902-1913 were abortive.

and perhaps not even a very important one. It is not impossible that the standard of commercial morality was higher in Scotland - certainly, there is little evidence of that brigandage or speculation in names detected by Shannon. Moreover, long before the legal changes of 1844 and 1855, Scots law had permitted joint stock enterprise for ordinary trading and manufacturing purposes that had been virtually prohibited to the English.[1] Largely because of the tolerant and liberal attitude adopted by the law in Scotland towards unincorporated concerns, the Scots had long enjoyed an acquaintance with business enterprise conducted with the aid of a form of organization the later introduction of which to England apparently gave rise to fraud and misrepresentation.[2] This familiarity may have made the potential Scottish investor more canny than his English counterpart and inhibited the activities of unscrupulous or inefficient company promoters. However, the statistics permit a diametrically opposite interpretation. An increase in the proportion of abortive companies in England between 1856 and 1865 suggested to Shannon that the rise might have been "due to greater caution among investors in taking up shares".[3] That is, to him a greater relative

---

1. H.A. Shannon, "The Coming of General Limited Liability", p.268: "Scotch /sic/ Law was different and better." R.H. Campbell, "The Law and the Joint-Stock Company in Scotland" in P.L. Payne (ed.), Studies in Scottish Business History (London: Cass 1967), pp.136-151, clearly shows both the differences and the superiority. See also A.B. DuBois, The English Business Company after the Bubble Act, 1720-1800 (New York: Octagon Books, 1971; a reprint of the almost unobtainable 1938 edition); and J. Robertson Christie, "Joint Stock Enterprise in Scotland before the Companies Acts", The Juridical Review, XXI (1909-1910), pp.128-147.

2. This should not be interpreted to mean that the Scots rigorously embraced joint stock enterprise at this period. The partnership remained supreme (see below, p.56). It was simply that the Scots appear not to have regarded joint stock with the acute suspicion so evident south of the border.

3. H.A. Shannon, "The First Five Thousand ...", p.402.

number of abortives might have been evidence of increasing care and calculation on the part of the investing public. It is improbable (for reasons set out later in this essay)[1] that such an explanation is plausible in the Scottish case.

Abortive companies were spread over every major field of activity. Only among the "Trade" and "Financial, Insurance and Real Estate" groups did they represent much more than 10 per cent of the promotions (compare Table 4 and Table 14). In "Agriculture, Forestry and Fishing" they were barely 3 per cent, and in "Manufacturing" which, by its miscellaneous and often technical nature, might have been expected to have presented the greatest opportunities for dishonesty, only 8.4 per cent.

With a relatively low abortion rate and a growing number of annual registration, the only factor which could prevent an increasing number of companies in existence was a low life expectancy. Since even those Scottish companies that had been dissolved by 1970 had an average length of life of 16.4 years (see Table 23), this condition did not apply. The result was that the number of Scottish firms in existence rose from eight in 1856 to 54 at the end of 1860, thence to 206 by December 1868. This figure almost doubled during the course of the boom years of the early 'seventies and had quadrupled by the end of the prosperous years of early 'eighties, only to double again by mid-1895 (see Chart 3). Although the latter part of this trend is similar to Todd's estimates for the United Kingdom as a whole,[2] it is probable that until the mid-'eighties the rate of increase in the number of Scottish companies in existence was

---

1. See below, pp.51-53.

2. Todd, op.cit., pp.62-63.

TABLE 6

NUMBER OF SCOTTISH COMPANIES IN EXISTENCE
YEAR END, 1856-1895

Year End	Number of Companies in Existence	Year End	Number of Companies in Existence
1856	8	1876	486
1857	31	1877	527
1858	37	1878	551
1859	42	1879	576
1860	54	1880	611
1861	73	1881	656
1862	101	1882	731
1863	122	1883	789
1864	134	1884	858
1865	162	1885	889
1866	188	1886	926
1867	193	1887	966
1868	206	1888	1030
1869	210	1889	1103
1870	224	1890	1192
1871	256	1891	1282
1872	328	1892	1374
1873	381	1893	1487
1874	425	1894	1606
1875	444	1895*	1755

*Estimated

No. Co.'s

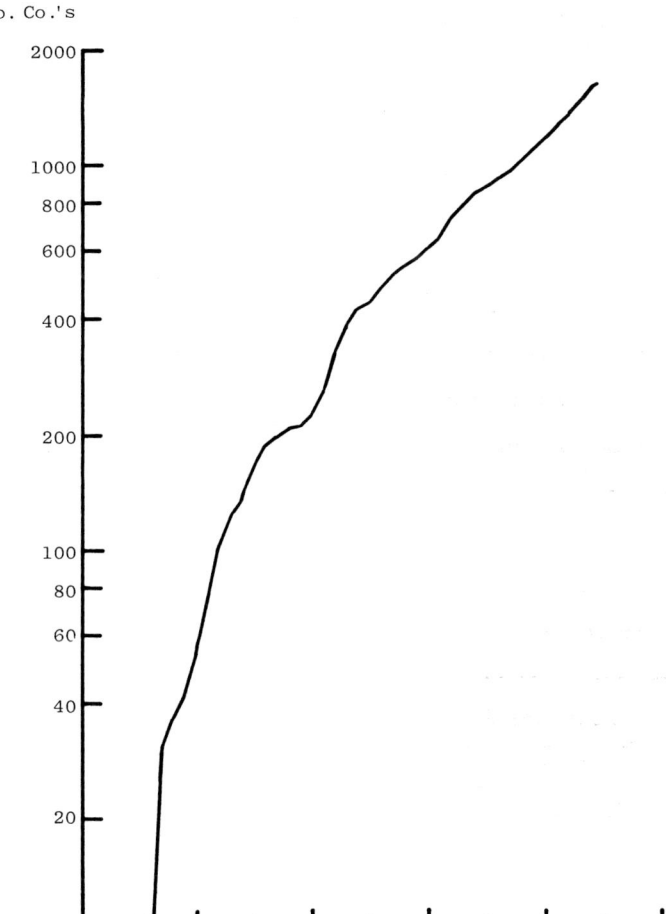

CHART 3: Number of Scottish Joint Stock Companies
in Existence at Year-End, 1856-1894

greater than that for English companies.[1] Certainly, it would appear
that the average length of life of the early Scottish companies (i.e.,
those incorporated before, say, the early 'eighties) was considerably
higher than that of the English companies. Even with the inclusion of
abortive companies (whose lives have been determined as anything from
still-birth - zero - to a few months) and the exclusion of companies
still in existence in 1960, the average length of life of Scottish
companies incorporated in any year before 1883 was only once (1856)
less than thirteen years (see Table 7). Admittedly, the use of the mean
figure conceals a wide distribution. Many companies enjoyed only a
brief existence, but what might be called the actuarial statistics for
Scottish companies create a different impression from those drawn from
early English experience. However disturbing the infantile mortality of
Scottish companies may have been, it was manifestly lower than that of
English companies. Levi's estimate of the average life of an English
company in 1865 was 18 months.[2] This is patently misleading, but even
Shannon's careful calculations reveal that of 2004 English companies in
existence in 1865 something over a quarter (27.7 per cent) and well over
one half (54.3 per cent) had died within 3 and 9 years, respectively.
For Scotland the comparable figures are but 16 per cent and 32.7 per cent.
Alternatively, of those English companies in existence in 1865, only a
quarter survived into the early 'nineties, whereas about a quarter of the

---

1. This observation is necessarily tentative because no reliable figures
   for English companies in existence are available. There are, for
   example, wide discrepancies between the Registrar's "official"
   figures and Todd's estimates.

2. Levi, J.R.S.S., 1870, p.17.

TABLE 7

AVERAGE LENGTH OF LIFE OF DISSOLVED SCOTTISH
COMPANIES BY YEAR OF BIRTH

Year of Birth	Number of Companies	Average Length of Life	
		Months	Years
1856	7	135.6	11.3
1857	22	233.6	19.5
1858	14	466.2	38.9
1859	5	568.2	47.4
1860	13	227.5	19.0
1861	22	315.2	26.3
1862	33	226.7	18.9
1863	28	178.8	14.9
1864	27	157.7	13.1
1865	36	213.8	17.8
1866	36	225.7	18.8
1867	17	230.0	13.5
1868	25	247.7	20.6
1869	17	330.4	27.5
1870	17	190.7	15.9
1871	43	253.1	21.1
1872	78	171.4	14.3
1873	58	190.5	15.9
1874	59	171.3	14.3
1875	45	225.5	18.8
1876	60	190.0	15.8
1877	78	220.8	18.4
1878	56	160.6	13.4
1879	52	182.5	15.2
1880	66	245.4	20.5
1881	71	224.7	18.7
1882	104	185.0	15.4
1883	105	159.6	13.3
1884	101	212.8	17.7
1885	72	175.2	14.6
1886	90	185.1	15.4
1887	82	221.6	18.5
1888	109	206.3	17.2
1889	122	196.6	16.4
1890	124	194.9	16.3
1891	135	174.3	14.5
1892	148	185.7	15.5
1893	169	186.5	15.5
1894	180	163.9	13.7
1895	99	181.7	15.1

Scottish companies of 1865 were still in existence on the eve of the First World War.[1] The full data are presented in Table 8 and Chart 4.[2]

Shannon found that "from 1865 the data of /survival of/ home companies /fitted a/, ... curve to the equation,

$$y = 1966. \; x^{-.65897}$$

and from 1886 to 1910 follow, with a slight fall-off in fit, a second ... curve to the equation,

$$y = 4677. \; x^{-1.0685"} \; [3]$$

In an attempt[4] to compare Shannon's findings with the Scottish data, a curve was fitted to figures recovered from his graph of survival for "home, foreign and colonial companies". For the period 1865-1886, this produced an equation

$$F = 2097. \; t^{-.60506} \qquad\qquad r^2 = 0.99$$
$$(0.03)$$

where F is the number of firms and t is time, and, for the period 1886-1928,

---

1. Cf. Todd, "Some Aspects ...", p.58, and Macgregor, "Joint Stock Companies ...", p.498.

2. The Scottish figures may give a more favourable actuarial impression than the English by the inclusion of relatively long-lived gas and water companies (see Table 23) specifically excluded by Shannon ("The First Five Thousand ...", pp.403-404), but this is partially, if not wholly, offset by the inclusion in the Scottish sample of abortive companies, a group omitted from Shannon's calculation of company survival.

3. Shannon, "The First Five Thousand ...", p.404.

4. For help in the following analysis, I am indebted to Professor Forrest D. Nelson.

THE SURVIVAL OF ENGLISH AND SCOTTISH COMPANIES
INCORPORATED BETWEEN 1856 AND 1865

Year End	Number of Companies in Existence — English	Number of Companies in Existence — Scottish	Percentage of Companies Surviving — English	Percentage of Companies Surviving — Scottish
1865	2004	162	100.0	100.0
1866		154		95.1
1867		143		88.3
1868	1449	136	72.3	84.0
1869		124		76.5
1870		122		75.3
1871	1101	120	54.9	74.1
1872		114		70.4
1873		113		69.8
1874	915	109	45.7	67.3
1875		105		64.8
1876		102		63.0
1877	795	97	39.7	59.9
1878		89		54.9
1879		87		53.7
1880	710	85	35.4	52.5
1881		84		51.9
1882		78		48.1
1883	640	72	31.9	44.4
1884		72		44.4
1885		72		44.4
1886	580	70	28.9	43.2
1887		70		43.2
1888		68		42.0
1889	520	67	25.9	41.4
1890		67		41.4
1891		67		41.4
1892	465	67	23.2	41.4
1893		66		40.7
1894		66		40.7
1895	440	64	22.0	39.5
1896		62		38.3
1897		61		37.7
1898	385	59	19.2	36.4
1899		56		34.6
1900		55		34.0
1901	345	50	17.2	30.9
1902		49		30.2
1903		49		30.2
1904	315	49	15.7	30.2
1905		47		29.0
1906		46		28.4
1907	300	43	15.0	26.5
1908		40		24.7
1909		40		24.7
1910	285	40	14.2	24.7
1911		40		24.7
1912		40		24.7
1913	260	39	13.0	24.1
1914		38		23.5
1915		38		23.5
1916	255	38	12.7	23.5
1917		37		22.8
1918		36		22.2
1919	250	35	12.5	21.6
1920		33		20.4
1921		33		20.4
1922	225	31	11.2	19.1
1923		30		18.5
1924		30		18.5
1925	205	30	10.2	18.5
1926		26		16.0
1927		25		15.4
1928	200	24	10.0	14.8
1931		23		14.2
1934		23		14.2
1937		20		12.3
1940	No Data	20	No Data	12.3
1950		15		9.3
1960		13		8.0
1970		13		8.0
1975		13		8.0

Note: The English data has been "recovered" from M. A. Shannon, "The First Five Thousand. . . ," Figure 1, p. 405, and may contain minor inaccuracies. The figures are those for "Home, Foreign and Colonial Companies," Graph 1.

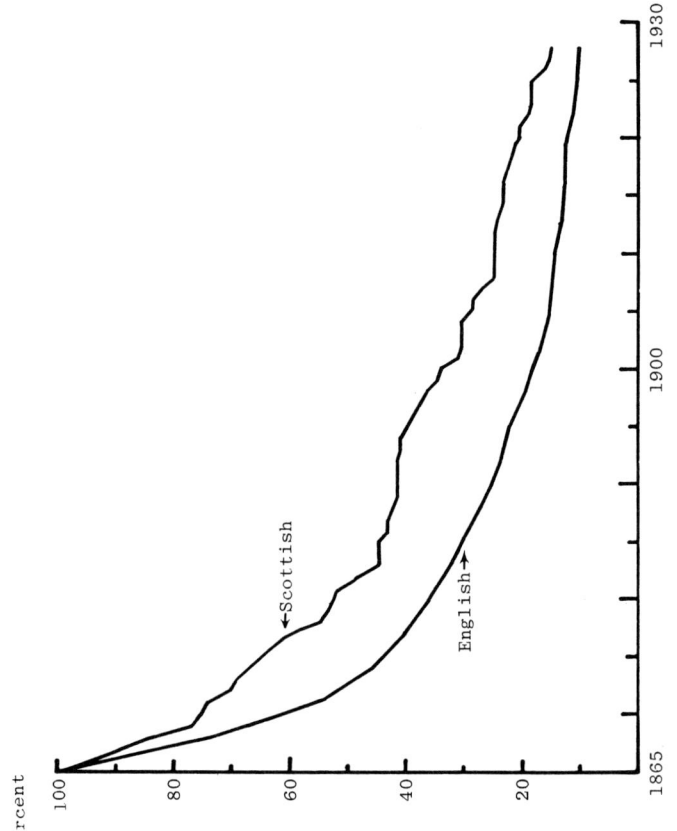

CHART 4: Percentage Survival of English and Scottish
Companies Incorporated between 1856 and 1865

$$F = 5291. \ t^{- \ 1.0563} \qquad\qquad r^2 = 0.99$$
$$(0.03)$$

Scottish data for all companies for the same periods fitted the following
equations:

For 1865–1886,
$$F = 1956. \ t^{- \ .2968} \qquad\qquad r^2 = 0.89$$

and for 1886–1928,
$$F = 1755. \ t^{- \ .9870} \qquad\qquad r^2 = 0.95$$

Because minor errors are inevitably introduced when trying to derive
values from a graph, no more is claimed from this analysis than that
it illustrates the hypotheses that (a) the rate of decay of the early
Scottish firms was far slower than for English firms; and (b) from the
mid-'eighties (that is, from the very time that Shannon's perceives a
break in the trend of survival displayed by English firms) the survival
trends of Scottish and English in existence in 1865 are very similar.

Graphs of survival of the Scottish firms in existence at the end
of 1865, 1885 and 1894 (Charts 4 and 5), derived from data in Tables 8
and 9, reveal that after a slight fall from 1865 to 1875 (explained by the
decreasing proportion of public utility companies) life expectancies had a
tendency to increase with the passage of years. After ten years, 58.8,
62.5 and 62.5 per cent of all Scottish companies in existence at the end
of 1875, 1885 and 1894, respectively, were still active; after twenty-five
years the proportions were 37.8, 38.8 and 41.2 per cent; after fifty years,
the proportions were 21.4, 25.9 and 27.7 per cent. By 1970, 11.0, 15.4 and
18.4 per cent of all companies in existence at the end of 1875, 1885 and

TABLE 9

THE SURVIVAL OF SCOTTISH COMPANIES IN EXISTENCE AT THE END OF 1875, 1885 and 1894

Year End	Number of Companies Incorporated since 1856 and Still in Existence at End of			Percentage of Companies Surviving of Those in Existence at End of		
	1875	1885	1894	1875	1885	1894
1875	444			100.0		
1876	421			94.8		
1877	387			87.2		
1878	361			81.3		
1879	343			77.3		
1880	321			72.3		
1881	306			68.9		
1882	293			66.0		
1883	275			61.9		
1884	266			59.9		
1885	261	889		58.8	100.0	
1886	249	839		56.1	94.4	
1887	244	792		55.0	89.1	
1888	235	749		52.9	84.3	
1889	229	710		51.6	79.9	
1890	222	674		50.0	75.8	
1891	216	647		48.6	72.8	
1892	213	629		48.0	70.8	
1893	211	608		47.5	68.4	
1894	205	581	1606	46.2	65.4	100.0
1895	197	556	1526	44.4	62.5	95.0
1896	193	530	1434	43.5	59.6	89.3
1897	186	515	1366	41.9	57.9	85.1
1898	178	495	1289	40.1	55.7	80.3
1899	171	475	1221	38.5	53.4	76.0
1900	168	464	1174	37.8	52.2	73.1
1901	158	444	1127	35.6	49.9	70.2
1902	150	426	1078	33.8	47.9	67.1
1903	149	419	1046	33.6	47.1	65.1
1904	141	401	1003	31.8	45.1	62.5
1905	140	395	974	31.5	44.4	60.6
1906	135	384	943	30.4	43.2	58.7
1907	131	366	908	29.5	41.2	56.5
1908	126	356	892	28.4	40.0	55.5
1909	126	350	845	28.4	39.4	52.6
1910	126	345	820	28.4	38.8	51.1
1911	124	337	800	27.9	37.9	49.8
1912	123	332	780	27.7	37.3	48.6
1913	121	329	769	27.3	37.0	47.9
1914	119	321	743	26.8	36.1	46.3
1915	117	318	734	26.4	35.8	45.7
1916	116	316	720	26.1	35.5	44.8
1917	113	313	695	25.5	35.2	43.3
1918	111	307	680	25.0	34.5	42.3
1919	108	299	662	24.3	33.6	41.2
1920	104	289	635	23.4	32.5	39.5
1921	100	285	619	22.5	32.1	38.5
1922	97	276	602	21.8	31.0	37.5
1923	94	269	586	21.2	30.3	36.5
1924	94	265	569	21.2	29.8	35.4
1925	94	264	564	21.2	29.7	35.1
1926	90	258	553	20.3	29.0	34.4
1927	89	254	548	20.0	28.6	34.1
1928	88	250	541	19.8	28.1	33.7
1929	87	248	537	19.6	27.9	33.4
1930	86	246	530	19.4	27.7	33.0
1931	86	242	522	19.4	27.2	32.5
1932	84	238	510	18.9	26.8	31.8
1933	83	234	505	18.7	26.3	31.4
1934	83	232	497	18.7	26.1	30.9
1935	83	230	493	18.7	25.9	30.7
1936	82	229	487	18.5	25.8	30.3
1937	79	220	471	17.8	24.7	29.3
1938	79	220	468	17.8	24.7	29.1
1939	79	220	464	17.8	24.7	28.9
1940	79	219	459	17.8	24.6	28.6
1941	78	215	455	17.6	24.2	28.3
1942	77	215	450	17.3	24.2	28.0
1943	77	213	448	17.3	24.0	27.9
1944	77	212	445	17.3	23.8	27.7
1945	77	207	438	17.3	23.3	27.3
1946	76	204	434	17.1	22.9	27.0
1947	76	203	427	17.1	22.8	26.6
1948	74	199	419	16.7	22.4	26.1
1949	62	176	382	14.0	19.8	23.8
1950	61	173	373	13.7	19.5	23.2
1951	61	171	369	13.7	19.2	23.0
1952	59	166	358	13.3	18.7	22.3
1953	58	162	349	13.1	18.2	21.7
1954	58	159	344	13.1	17.9	21.4
1955	55	155	336	12.4	17.4	20.9
1956	55	155	335	12.4	17.4	20.9
1957	55	153	332	12.4	17.2	20.7
1958	55	150	327	12.4	16.9	20.4
1959	55	149	323	12.4	16.7	20.1
1960	55	149	318	12.4	16.7	19.8
1961	53	144	311	11.9	16.2	19.4
1962	51	140	307	11.5	15.7	19.1
1963	51	140	303	11.5	15.7	18.9
1964	50	138	301	11.3	15.5	18.7
1965	49	138	301	11.0	15.5	18.7
1966	49	138	299	11.0	15.5	18.6
1967	49	137	298	11.0	15.4	18.6
1968	49	137	298	11.0	15.4	18.6
1969	49	137	298	11.0	15.4	18.6
1970	49	137	296	11.0	15.4	18.4
1971	49	137	296	11.0	15.4	18.4
1972	49	137	296	11.0	15.4	18.4
1973	49	137	296	11.0	15.4	18.4
1974	49	137	296	11.0	15.4	18.4
1975	49	137	296	11.0	15.4	18.4

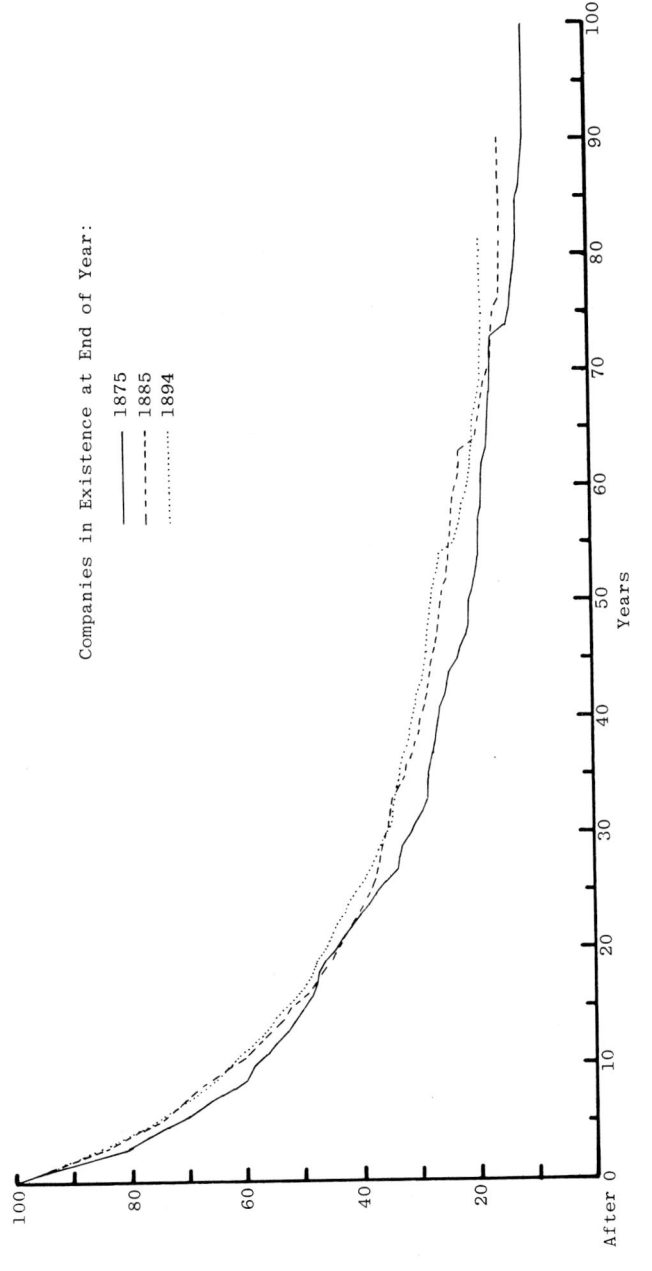

Percent

Companies in Existence at End of Year:

——— 1875
– – – 1885
········· 1894

Years

After 0   10   20   30   40   50   60   70   80   90   100

CHART 5: Percentage Survival of Scottish Companies in
Existence at End of Years 1875, 1885 and 1894

1894 remained in operation in their original form, despite the relatively heavy mortality occasioned by nationalization in the late 1940's. Furthermore, not all of the Scottish companies that were dissolved passed entirely out of existence. Of the 2157 companies incorporated between 1856 to mid-1895 which had been wound up by the end of 1914, just over 16 per cent (351) had been dissolved for sale, reconstruction and amalgamation (Table 4, Mode of Dissolution Type 2, and Table 10). Of these, something over one half, or about 10 per cent of all dissolutions, were as a consequence of sale to or merger with existing companies (many of them incorporated in England), approximately double the proportion that Macgregor found for the London registrations of 1880.[1]

With the exception of Macgregor's analysis of the survival of English companies incorporated in 1880,[2] no strictly comparable figures for England exist.[3] Of these 1162 companies, Macgregor omitted from consideration 54 wound up for amalgamation, five transferred to public authorities, and 27 for which there was inadequate information. Taking only those 780 English companies "effectively formed" (i.e., omitting 296 abortive companies), and using Macgregor's form of tabulation and methods (i.e., omitting abortives and companies dissolved for the purpose of amalgamation) to treat the 70 Scottish firms incorporated in 1880, produces the survival statistics presented in Table 11. These data simply

---

1. Macgregor, op.cit., p.494.

2. Ibid., pp.494-5.

3. Although A. Essex-Crosby does mention that "in 1885 the number of companies on the register in England and Scotland was 8,924 .... Between 1862 and 1884, 8,021 had been eliminated by compulsory orders for liquidation, whilst a further 5,435 had been voluntarily wound up or had been struck off the registers as defunct; the survivors thus represented 40 per cent of the registrations". A. Essex-Crosby, Joint-Stock Companies in Great Britain, p.24.

TABLE 10

AN INDUSTRIAL CLASSIFICATION OF SCOTTISH COMPANIES WHICH
WERE DISSOLVED BEFORE 1914 BY BEING "SOLD, AMALGAMATED
OR RECONSTRUCTED"* BY MAJOR INDUSTRIAL GROUPS

Industrial Classification Number	Brief Description	Number of Companies	Proportion of Total
100	Mining and Quarrying	40	11.7
200-300	Manufacturing	125	36.4
400	Public Utilities	78	22.7
500-600	Trade	16	4.7
700	Service	25	7.3
800	Finance, Insurance and Real Estate	51	14.9
900	Agriculture, Foresting and Fishing	8	2.3
	Total	343	100.0

*Mode of dissolution Type 2

TABLE 11

SURVIVAL OF ENGLISH AND SCOTTISH COMPANIES FORMED IN 1880

Period	Number of Companies		Percentage Survival of Companies	
	English (780)	Scottish (56)	English	Scottish
1 year	720	55	92	98
2 years	636	54	82	96
5 years	456	44	58	79
10 years	333	34	43	61
20 years	233	25	30	45
30 years	173	19	22	34
40 years	145	15	19	27
49 years	126	13	16	23

Source of English data: D. H. Macgregor, "Joint Stock Companies. . . .",
pp. 493-95. Of the 70 Scottish companies incorporated in 1880, 7 were
abortive and 7 were dissolved for amalgamation.

confirm the greater longevity of the early Scottish companies, but on
the basis of Todd's estimates one would guess that after the mid-'eighties
the survival trends of English companies were becoming increasingly
similar to those of the Scottish companies; that three decades of intensive
experience with the joint-stock limited liability form of business
organization had placed English promoters, directors and investors on a
footing more nearly equal to their initially more knowledgeable and
prudent counterparts north of the border.

But is there more to explaining the greater stability of the early
Scottish joint-stock companies than simply the Scots' greater familiarity
with this organizational form? Todd argues that not until the limitation
of liability became effective, that is, not until the proportion of
uncalled capital was significantly reduced, was "a better and more
efficient class of entrepreneurs" encouraged "to enter industry" with a
resultant rise in the standard of commercial morality and decrease in
fraud.[1] If this argument is sound, it would partially explain the
increasing longevity of English companies during the course of the century.
But all those hypotheses that are dependent on presumed changes in the
ratio of called to nominal capital have hitherto rested upon very tenuous
data. It is not enough to cite Giffen's observation that "since 1866
there have been few companies with large amounts of uncalled capital, the
special evil of the pre-1866 period",[2] when the Parliamentary Returns

---

1. Todd, op.cit., pp.67-68.

2. Giffen, Economic Inquiries and Studies, p.120, quoted by Todd,
   op.cit., p.69.

- 45 -

reveal that in only three years between 1866 and 1882 did the total paid-up capital of companies in the Registrar's sample exceed 30 per cent of their nominal capital.[1] That the official returns - vitiated as they were by the inclusion of large numbers of abortive companies which until 1880 the Registrar was unable to remove, and often dependent for their compilation upon dubious information supplied by companies - are unreliable is recognised, but they do indicate that the effective limitation of liability occurred much later than is sometimes supposed. Taking _all_ the companies given in _Burdett's Official Intelligence_ the proportion of paid-up to issued capital was 60 per cent in 1885 and 67 per cent in 1895. Sectorially, the lowest proportions of paid-up to issued capital in 1885 were in the groups "Finance, Land and Investment" (61 per cent), "Banking" (24.6 per cent) and "Insurance" (21.8 per cent).[2] In Scotland, after the first seven years of the operation of the Act of 1856, the proportion of called-up to nominal capital of all active companies registered in Edinburgh before 1895 never exceeded 50 per cent,[3] though a strong upward tendency in this ratio is apparent from the early 'eighties (see Table 12). Certainly, it was from this date that there was mounting criticism in Scotland of the

---

1. This statement is based on figures kindly supplied to my by Philip Cottrell.

2. Jefferys, _Business Organization_, Appendix D, pp.456-57, based on A. Essex-Crosby, _Joint-Stock Companies in Great Britain_, pp.220-21. For Essex-Crosby's discussion of unpaid liability on issued capital, see pp.26-32.

3. It should perhaps be mentioned that there is a technical difference between the proportion of called-up to (a) issued (or subscribed) capital and to (b) nominal capital. Several Scottish companies (and I suspect numerous English companies) were unable to, or chose not to, issue shares to the full extent of their nominal capital. Thus, in aggregate terms, the proportion called/nominal capital always falls short of the proportion called/issued capital. Whether this fact is sufficient to explain the difference between the proportions given in my Table 12 and those given by A. Essex-Crosby is not known.

TABLE 12

CAPITAL OF SCOTTISH JOINT STOCK COMPANIES IN EXISTENCE AT YEAR END, 1856-1895

Year End	Capital of Companies Dissolved before 1975			All Companies
	Nominal (£s)	Called Up (£s)	$\frac{\text{Called Up}}{\text{Nominal}}$(%)	Called Up (£000s) (Estimated)
1856	554,400	321,410	58.0	321
1857	2,293,630	456,629	19.9	488
1858	370,080	250,800	67.8	258
1859	397,330	256,968	64.7	257
1860	476,230	294,605	61.9	301
1861	573,450	330,106	57.6	371
1862	5,932,450	2,966,046	50.0	3,221
1863	6,921,370	3,445,518	49.8	3,787
1864	8,246,158	3,616,117	43.9	4,005
1865	11,324,072	4,243,337	37.5	4,645
1866	15,365,685	4,839,272	31.5	5,289
1867	15,855,897	5,112,836	32.2	5,639
1868	16,360,190	6,108,225	37.3	6,486
1869	16,261,607	6,526,118	40.1	7,251
1870	16,659,546	6,736,323	40.4	7,507
1871	18,035,641	7,231,159	40.1	7,811
1872	23,497,972	9,453,833	40.2	10,441
1873	26,109,278	11,377,268	43.6	12,601
1874	29,699,276	12,820,061	43.2	14,726
1875	34,639,725	14,789,733	42.7	16,417
1876	36,257,358	15,016,551	41.4	16,972
1877	38,059,449	14,727,589	38.7	16,479
1878	38,338,301	14,083,659	36.7	15,773
1879	38,056,404	13,957,213	36.7	16,576
1880	42,096,359	15,279,009	36.3	17,816
1881	52,889,509	16,641,587	31.5	19,322
1882	73,013,601	20,616,897	28.2	24,037
1883	75,617,910	24,034,710	31.8	28,052
1884	73,537,263	25,983,668	35.3	30,415
1885	74,105,987	27,602,676	37.2	32,502
1886	78,341,431	29,183,141	37.3	34,164
1887	80,565,703	30,053,829	37.3	35,798
1888	85,457,151	32,474,066	38.0	38,624
1889	84,026,240	33,426,940	39.8	39,989
1890	88,418,806	36,101,510	40.8	43,076
1891	81,366,433	34,729,874	42.7	41,964
1892	85,115,531	38,188,173	44.9	45,866
1893	87,574,694	40,869,177	46.7	49,409
1894	91,094,045	43,543,598	47.8	52,738
1895	92,094,077	45,602,589	49.5	55,752

practice of issuing debenture bonds on the security of uncalled capital.
The property and finance companies were particular offenders. As Lawson
remarked: "Directors who trade on uncalled capital say in effect to
depositors and debenture holders - 'If we mismanage this business and lose
your money, we have a lot of unsophisticated old ladies behind us, whom
you can sell up to the last chair or table they have got'."[1]

Until more empirical studies have been undertaken into the London
registrations, the stability of English companies will remain obscure.
In the Scottish case, much remains to be done with the data available
at West Register House, Edinburgh, but if the effort already expended
may be held to justify further speculation, it is possible that the
relatively low Scottish abortion rate, the longer lives of companies
registered in Edinburgh, and the apparently[2] higher standards of commercial
morality extant in late nineteenth century Scotland, might be explained
in terms of the more intimate nature of the Scottish financial scene.
London's money market approached the anonymity postulated by the economist
more nearly than those in Scotland. In Edinburgh, Glasgow, Dundee and
Aberdeen, promoters, business men and investors were more likely to be
acquainted not only with each other but with the motives and prospects of

---

1. W.R. Lawson, The Scottish Investors' Manual: A Review of the Leading
   Scottish Securities in 1883 (Edinburgh & London: William Blackwood &
   Sons, 1884), pp.22-3. The article from which this quotation is taken,
   "On Uncalled Capital as a Borrowing Medium", was said to have first
   appeared in The Edinburgh Courant.

2. I use the word "apparently" because it is difficult, if not, in the
   overwhelming majority of cases, impossible, to prove fraud and
   misrepresentation from the information in the company files, even
   in those cases which arouse justifiable suspicions.

the companies which jostled for their attention.[1] The same names repeatedly

occur among the signatories of the Articles of Association, the occupations

of the shareholders frequently indicate some connection with the type of

activity proposed in the company's objectives. Even those who withdrew

their nest eggs from the Savings Bank of Glasgow to put them into concerns

engaged in cattle-raising or mining half a world away often did so on the

basis of advice or information contained in letters from relatives or

friends who had previously emigrated to the very areas in which the concerns

proposed to operate.[2] Yet the share denominations of Scottish companies

(Table 13) provide little evidence that any real attempt was made to appeal

to the small man. Whereas over time there is a marked increase in the

---

1. This raises the question of whether Scotland was simply one local market
    among several. Similar results might emerge from a parallel inquiry -
    were it possible - of, say, the capital markets of Liverpool or
    Manchester. Could it be that the comparisons made in this study are
    local/national rather than Scottish/English? I am indebted to Don
    McCloskey for drawing my attention to this point. Certainly as Kennedy
    has emphasized, "provincial exchanges ... were essentially an extension
    of the close circle of associates /who had always supplied industrial
    capital in Britain/ since those who traded in local markets were
    generally well aware of the circumstances of the firms quoted there".
    W.P. Kennedy, "Institutional Response to Economic Growth: Capital
    Markets in Britain to 1914", in Les Hannah (ed.), Management Strategy
    and Business Development (London: Macmillan, 1976), p.162.

2. Dr. Michie shows that "it was not so much the blind pursuit of the
    highest interest rates that drew Scottish capital to the furthest
    corners of the world, but an intricate network of local, personal and
    business relationships which channelled available funds into the
    profitable opportunities recognised by expatriate Scots. Investors
    felt a sense of kin with these expatriates and so were willing to trust
    them with a part of their wealth which would not have been readily
    released to an anonymous foreigner, no matter the interest paid or
    the gain promised". Michie, op.cit., p.473. In the case of Australia,
    the whole process has been remarkably illustrated by David Macmillan,
    see his Scotland and Australia, 1788-1850 (Oxford: Oxford University
    Press, 1967), passim, but especially pp.326-63. See also: Paul M.
    Edwards, The Scottish Role in Midland America with Special Reference
    to Wyoming, 1865-1895 (University of St. Andrews: unpublished Ph.D.
    thesis, 1972), p.287; J.D. Bailey, "Australian Borrowing in Scotland
    in the Nineteenth Century", Economic History Review, 2nd Series, XII
    (1959-60), pp.268-79.

TABLE 13

SHARE DENOMINATIONS OF SCOTTISH COMPANIES, 1856-1895

December of Year	Number of Companies	(1) Up to and Including £1		(2) £1+ - £5		(3) £5+ - £10		(4) £10+ - £25		(5) £25+ - £50		(6) £50+ - £99.99		(7) £100 and Over	
		Number	%	Number	%	Number	%	Number	%	Number	%	Number	%	Number	%
1856	7	1	14.3	1	14.3	-	-	1	14.3	2	28.6	-	-	2	28.6
1857	29	1	3.4	10	35.5	1	3.4	6	20.7	3	10.3	3	10.3	5	17.2
1858	36	4	11.1	14	38.9	5	13.9	5	13.9	2	5.6	2	5.6	4	11.1
1859	39	4	10.3	15	38.5	7	17.9	5	12.8	2	5.1	2	5.1	4	10.3
1860	48	4	8.3	19	39.6	7	14.6	8	16.7	1	2.1	4	8.3	5	10.4
1861	65	6	9.2	27	41.5	12	18.5	9	13.8	2	3.1	4	6.2	5	7.7
1862	93	9	9.7	38	40.9	19	20.4	11	11.8	3	3.2	5	5.4	8	8.6
1863	111	10	9.0	46	41.4	22	19.8	14	12.6	4	3.6	4	3.6	11	9.9
1864	121	10	8.3	47	38.8	22	18.2	20	16.5	4	3.3	4	3.3	14	11.6
1865	148	10	6.8	52	35.1	30	20.3	28	18.9	3	2.0	7	4.7	18	12.2
1866	172	11	6.4	58	33.7	29	16.9	36	20.9	5	2.9	9	5.2	24	14.0
1867	175	10	5.7	59	33.7	33	18.9	34	19.4	6	3.4	9	5.1	24	13.7
1868	194	12	6.2	68	35.1	33	17.0	38	18.6	6	3.1	10	5.2	29	14.9
1869	189	11	5.8	70	37.0	28	14.8	30	15.9	8	4.2	12	6.3	30	15.9
1870	201	10	5.0	76	37.8	29	14.4	30	14.9	9	4.5	14	7.0	33	16.4
1871	237	11	4.6	88	37.1	39	16.5	42	17.7	11	4.6	14	5.9	32	13.5
1872	297	13	4.4	98	33.0	47	15.8	72	24.2	14	4.7	17	5.7	36	12.1
1873	344	15	4.4	108	31.4	56	16.3	91	26.5	15	4.4	16	4.7	43	12.5
1874	370	16	4.3	109	29.5	64	17.3	106	28.6	16	4.3	17	4.6	42	11.4
1875	400	16	4.0	115	28.7	78	19.5	115	28.7	15	3.7	17	4.2	44	11.0
1876	430	18	4.2	116	27.0	86	20.0	131	30.5	18	4.2	16	3.7	45	10.5
1877	471	21	4.5	127	27.0	93	19.7	154	32.7	16	3.4	15	3.2	45	9.6
1878	492	24	4.9	134	27.2	99	20.1	164	33.3	15	3.0	14	2.8	42	8.5
1879	485	25	5.2	136	28.0	93	19.2	161	33.2	17	3.5	14	2.9	39	8.0
1880	524	26	5.0	152	29.0	104	19.8	173	33.0	17	3.2	13	2.5	39	7.4
1881	565	29	5.1	169	29.9	106	18.8	187	33.1	18	3.2	15	2.7	41	7.3
1882	627	38	6.1	174	27.8	123	19.6	214	34.1	17	2.7	18	2.9	43	6.9
1883	676	40	5.9	180	26.6	139	20.6	230	34.0	17	2.5	20	3.0	50	7.4
1884	733	46	6.3	199	27.1	154	21.0	241	32.9	17	2.3	20	2.7	56	7.6
1885	755	44	5.8	210	27.8	163	21.6	240	31.8	18	2.4	21	2.8	59	7.8
1886	791	43	5.4	225	28.4	168	21.2	249	31.5	23	2.9	21	2.7	62	7.8
1887	811	44	5.4	231	28.5	172	21.6	257	31.7	22	2.7	23	2.8	62	7.6
1888	866	44	5.1	260	30.0	174	20.1	273	31.5	22	2.5	24	2.8	69	8.0
1889	922	42	4.6	290	31.5	177	19.2	287	31.1	21	2.3	30	3.3	75	8.1
1890	999	45	4.5	311	31.1	185	18.5	315	31.5	24	2.4	36	3.6	83	8.3
1891	1061	49	4.6	325	30.6	195	18.6	329	31.0	26	2.5	41	3.9	96	9.0
1892	1144	53	4.6	345	30.2	200	17.5	367	32.1	28	2.4	44	3.8	107	9.4
1893	1230	52	4.2	374	30.4	206	16.7	402	32.7	27	2.2	51	4.1	118	9.6
1894	1326	53	4.0	420	31.7	221	16.7	419	31.6	25	1.9	59	4.4	129	9.7
1895	1339	50	3.7	427	31.9	222	16.6	429	32.0	24	1.8	59	4.4	128	9.6

Note: Any apparent inconsistencies between the number of companies for which data is provided in this table (all of which had been dissolved by 1975) and the number of companies in existence on the last day of each calendar year (see Table) is explained by the fact that data are here provided for every company which enjoyed an existence during some part of the last month of

proportion of English companies offering shares in £1 or less, or from
£1 to £5,[1] in Scotland, throughout the period 1875-1895, the most popular
denomination was in the £10+ to £25 range and a significantly higher
proportion of total capital was raised north of the border by shares of
an even larger denomination. The £1 share made relatively little headway
in Scotland except as a means of raising capital for public halls, social
clubs, co-operative groups of artisans and small concerns which Shannon,
for example, omits from his analysis, though the £1 - £5 share, initially
more widely used in Scotland than in England, remained highly important
throughout the period under consideration.[2]

Scotland's financial world was apparently tight-knit. As Dr. Michie
has observed, "Most Scottish stock exchanges continued to retain, in the
second half of the nineteenth century, a long list of local joint-stock
companies whose shares were held locally and interest in which was largely
confined to one area. Concerns as diverse as the Glasgow and South-
Western Railway, the City of Glasgow Bank, the Scottish American Investment
Company, and the Matador Land and Cattle Company, all drew most of their
investors from one particular area not Scotland as a whole ... each major
town or city had its own individual joint-stock concerns in a wide range
of activities. For example, there were, by 1899, almost 200 public
companies with a paid-up capital of £203m, whose headquarters were in and

---

1. Shannon, "The Limited Companies of 1866-1883", p.300. An unpublished
    table of English "Share Denominations, 1856-1882", prepared by Philip
    Cottrell, provides much more detailed information.

2. It is perhaps worth emphasizing, as Professor S.G. Checkland has
    pointed out in a letter to the author, that the existence of the £1
    note, general in Scotland but absent in England, had long accustomed
    the people to small denomination paper. See his Scottish Banking:
    A History, 1695-1973, passim, but especially pp.435-9.

around Glasgow. A similar situation existed for the other major Scottish
cities, especially Edinburgh and Aberdeen. Even in a field such as overseas
investment each city had its own concerns. Whereas Dundee investors
channelled their investment in North America through such concerns as the
Scottish America Investment Trust and the Alliance Trust Company, Aberdeen
investors utilized such ventures as the Texas Land and Mortgage Company,
the Colorado Land and Mortgage Company, and the North of Scotland Canadian
Mortgage Company".[1] Evidence elsewhere indicates an awareness of plans and
projects by members of the commercial and industrial community that is
surprisingly well informed and sophisticated.[2] Small investors may, on
occasion have been gullible, but they were not stupid. Even small
savings were moved about to obtain the highest yield[3] and because many
investors earned a living - few are described as "gentlemen" - they were
perhaps better able to assess the practicability of the schemes put before
them than their English counterparts. Hence promoters, or those seeking
to convert partnerships into companies, or those wishing to "work a patent"
had to present credible projects to the public, and even then a local
connection was all but imperative.[4] This made for relatively few

---

1. R.C. Michie, op.cit., p.409-10.

2. P.L. Payne, Colvilles and the Scottish Steel Industry (Oxford:
   Clarendon Press, 1979), passim.

3. P.L. Payne, "The Savings Bank of Glasgow, 1836-1914", in Payne (ed.),
   Studies in Scottish Business History, pp.173-80.

4. Dr. Michie found that of 1,650 companies that appealed for capital
   through a public prospectus inserted in the Aberdeen press over the
   period 1845-95, only 166 were apparently successful in raising capital
   in Aberdeen. Yet of the 111 companies operating in the north-east of
   Scotland that sought support through the Aberdeen press, "a total of
   65 (59 per cent) were successful. Similarly, of the 73 companies
   operating outside the region but in which well-known local figures were
   involved, a total of 31 (42 per cent) were successful. Overall, a
   'local' company had a 52 per cent chance of attracting investment from
   north-east Scotland while a non-local concern had only a 4 per cent
   chance". Michie, op.cit., pp.447-8.

abortions and a higher ratio of successful flotations than occurred in England. It also made for more stable companies.

The Scots apparently even resisted the urge to invest in dubious projects promoted during periods of unusual optimism. The hypothesis was tested that companies incorporated during periods of cyclical upswing might be less carefully planned than those projected during depression years. It was expected that the former, feverishly spawned during boom conditions, might carry a taint from birth which would make itself manifest in a relatively short life; that during the growing excitement of an upswing the habitual prudence of the Scottish investor might have been swept aside. This idea proved to have no foundation: if anything, companies formed during upswings enjoyed a slightly longer length of life than those incorporated during downswings.[1]

III

FIELDS OF ENTERPRISE

The incorporation of joint stock limited companies under the Act of 1856 got off to a slow start in Scotland. For many years this form of business organization was mainly confined to the public utilities, particularly to the provision of gas, light and water (where several companies represented simple conversions of co-partnerships formed earlier in the century[2]), and to shipping. A harbinger of later events was the

---

1. The investigation was based on data presented in Table 7.

2. For example, The Falkirk Joint Stock Gas Co. Ltd. had originally been constituted as a co-partnery in May, 1845.

TABLE 14

AN INDUSTRIAL CLASSIFICATION OF SCOTTISH JOINT STOCK COMPANIES
INCORPORATED BETWEEN 1856 AND MID-1895, BY MAJOR INDUSTRIAL GROUPS

Year	100 Mining & Quarrying	200-300 Manufacturing	400 Public Utilities	500-600 Trade	700 Service	800 Finance, Insurance, & Real Estate	900 Agriculture, Forestry, & Fishing	Total
1856	-	3	5	-	-	-	-	8
1857	1	7	8	3	1	1	2	23
1858	1	2	10	-	1	-	-	14
1859	-	-	5	-	1	-	-	6
1860	3	3	7	-	-	1	1	15
1861	5	5	11	3	-	-	-	24
1862	6	3	14	1	1	7	2	34
1863	3	4	10	-	2	9	3	31
1864	1	4	14	2	2	4	-	27
1865	1	12	13	-	1	5	6	38
1866	3	16	12	3	-	2	2	38
1867	-	2	10	2	2	1	1	18
1868	5	2	10	2	2	3	1	25
1869	1	-	9	1	2	2	4	19
1870	2	3	6	-	2	5	1	19
1871	4	13	17	4	2	6	2	48
1872	18	26	20	4	5	9	3	85
1873	17	16	12	2	7	6	3	63
1874	8	11	16	4	6	17	4	66
1875	6	9	11	4	6	12	-	48
1876	9	15	15	2	6	18	4	69
1877	5	15	17	3	19	27	2	88
1878	4	13	10	3	18	15	1	64
1879	6	9	15	3	15	14	3	65
1880	2	20	12	5	16	12	3	70
1881	7	22	21	2	8	14	2	76
1882	8	24	36	2	8	24	12	114
1883	8	35	32	6	14	14	8	117
1884	10	43	23	4	13	12	8	113
1885	6	24	16	3	7	13	9	78
1886	8	31	19	5	10	15	5	93
1887	7	30	20	9	12	16	3	97
1888	9	41	29	9	13	21	3	125
1889	20	47	35	3	14	15	3	137
1890	17	59	32	7	10	16	7	148
1891	7	65	40	7	21	14	3	157
1892	13	64	38	9	21	13	6	164
1893	21	70	46	10	15	20	7	189
1894	27	65	54	10	24	23	4	207
1895	18	49	20	2	13	9	5	116
Total	297	882	750	139	320	415	133	2,936
%	10.0	30.0	25.6	4.7	10.9	14.1	4.5	100.0

North British Rubber Co., but it was hardly typical. Established in 1857 by American enterprise to exploit Charles Goodyear's Scottish patent for the manufacture of india-rubber,[1] it was the earliest example of that trans-Atlantic inflow of capital and technological expertise that has so stimulated the Scottish economy in recent years.[2] Not until the mid-'sixties, and then only as a temporary efflorescence, was there any significant movement into industrial activity. In 1866, two years after the expiration of James "Paraffin" Young's patent for the process, no fewer than nine companies were floated for the extraction and distillation of mineral oil, but with the exception of Young's own company (itself a successor to a co-partnery formed in 1850)[3] and the Capeldrae Oil and Coal Co. Ltd., which survived into the late 'seventies, all had been wound up within a few years. Other branches of manufacturing activity experienced little more than a twinge of the limited urge before the 'seventies. A

---

1. For the North British Rubber Co., see W. Woodruff, "The American Origins of a Scottish Industry", Scottish Journal of Political Economy, Vol.II (1955), pp.17-32; W. Woodruff, The Rise of the British Rubber Industry During the Nineteenth Century (Liverpool: Liverpool University Press, 1958), pp.143, 154, 210-11. John Dunning, American Investment in British Manufacturing Industry (London: Allen & Unwin, 1958), p.17, states that this is the first American venture in British manufacturing industry. In fact, it is the second, Samuel Colt's London factory for the production of fire arms having preceded it five years earlier. Mira Wilkins, The Emergence of Multinational Enterprise: American Business Abroad from the Colonial Era to 1914 (Cambridge, Massachusetts: Harvard University Press, 1970), pp.30, 259.

2. David J.C. Forsyth, U.S. Investment in Scotland (New York: Praeger, 1972).

3. For "Paraffin" Young, see W.H. Marwick, "The Limited Company in Scottish Economic Development", Economic History, Vol.IV (1937), p.416, and John Butt, "The Scottish Oil Mania of 1864-6", Scottish Journal of Political Economy, XII (1965), pp.195-209.

few bakery firms, operating with small capitals of £1000 or less, a pottery, a railway carriage and wagon builder, one or two newspaper publishers: the list is short and unimpressive. In mining and quarrying, joint stock ventures under the Act of 1856 initially represented little more than short-lived speculations in copper and silver lead.

A number of banks, already in being under contracts of co-partnery, registered with unlimited liability in 1862.[1] Among them were the Union Bank, the Aberdeen Town and Country Bank, the ill-fated City of Glasgow Bank, the Caledonian, the North of Scotland Banking Co., and the Clydesdale. In "Finance, Insurance and Real Estate", they were joined in the following year by a number of insurance companies, the longest lived of which was destined to be the British Legal Life Assurance and Loan Co., but thereafter the group was quiescent until the 'seventies. Only with public utilities did the adoption of the joint stock limited liability form of organization sustain any momentum.

Not until the great boom of the early 'seventies can there be discerned any significant relaxation of the grip of the partnership. Forty-eight companies were incorporated in Scotland in 1871 and 85 in 1872, a two- to three-fold increase over any previous year. Companies involved in coal mining and iron-making led the way.[2] A need for fixed capital beyond the accumulated wealth of the founders and their successors, many of whom wished to withdraw from active participation in the firms that had been instrumental in creating their fortunes, coupled with a

---

1. For the general context, see S.G. Checkland, Scottish Banking: A History, 1695-1973 (Glasgow: Collins, 1975), Chapter 15, pp.463-97.

2. For the intimate connection between these activities in Scotland, see P.L. Payne, Colvilles ..., pp.45-55.

desire to reduce their financial responsibilities when the inevitable
reaction to the boom set in,[1] brought about the creation of such limited
companies as the Benhar Coal Co., the Lochore and Capledrae Cannel Coal
Co., the Rawyards Coal Co., the Fife Coal Co., the Flemington Coal Co.,
and the Cairntable Gas Coal Co., and, primarily in iron, the Monkland
Iron and Coal Co., the Omoa and Cleland Iron and Coal Co., Merry and
Cunninghame, William Dixon and the Blochairn Iron Co. Most of these were
conversions, the vendors taking a relatively high proportion of the share
capital. George Simpson, who sold his colliery interests to the Benhar
Coal Co., of which he became managing director, was partially recompensed
by having 25 per cent of the firm's nominal capital of £20,000 issued
to him in the form of 500 fully paid £10 shares;[2] George Willis, a co-
partner of Andrew Yeats and Co., the vendors, received £3000 in cash, 1000
fully paid £10 shares and 2000 shares of the same denomination, of which
£6 was deemed to have been paid, in the Gartcraig Coal and Fireclay Co.;
Thomas Barr, David Ingles Urquhart and Hugh McKinnell, were allotted
2000 £10 shares fully paid (or 40 per cent of the nominal capital) in the
Cairntable Gas Coal Co., to whom they sold their colliery interests in
1873; William Smith Dixon received £388,000 for the sale of Dixon's
Ironworks, over half of which he received in the form of £1000 shares in

---

1. These reasons are discussed more fully in J.B. Jefferys, Business
   Organisation, pp.76-84.

2. In 1874 the Benhar Coal Co. amalgamated with the Niddrie Coal Co.
   less than six months after the latter's incorporation. The Niddrie,
   like the Benhar, represented the conversion of George Simpson's
   colliery interests. As vendor, Simpson received 7,810 £10 shares
   (£2 paid) in the Niddrie. The merged concern nearly foundered in
   1879 when George Simpson went bankrupt "amid charges of maladministra-
   tion, if not malversation". Marwick, op.cit., p.418.

William Dixon Ltd. W.S. Dixon, grandson of the first William Dixon, the profits of whose collieries had established the family fortune at the turn of the century, wished to devote less attention to the vast and ramified family business created by his vigorous predecessors.[1] Similarly, James Merry, who with Alexander Cunninghame, was proprietor of the Glengarnock Iron Co. and collieries throughout Lanarkshire, became by far the largest shareholder in Merry and Cunninghame when that company was incorporated in 1872.[2] As Jefferys has explained, James Merry's reasons for selling out to a limited company were made quite explicit in the prospectus:

> "Mr. Cunninghame died in 1865 ... the present contract of co-partnery expires in 1879 and Mr. Cunninghame's Trustees who are bound to realise his estate as speedily as possible, must withdraw his capital from the business at the earliest opportunity. Mr. Merry does not feel disposed to add to the large interest which he already holds in the undertaking and as neither of his sons desires to engage in commercial pursuits he prefers gradually to withdraw from active business. It would be almost impossible to find private capitalists to contribute the capital necessary for such an enterprise and it has therefore been resolved to place the present proposal before the public."[3]

Conversions took place elsewhere in the heavy industries. Tod and McGregor, the Partick shipbuilders, went limited in January 1872, the Govan

---

1. For the activities of the earlier members of the Dixon family, see Henry Hamilton, The Industrial Revolution in Scotland (Oxford: Oxford University Press, 1932), pp.173, 184, 186, 196; P.L. Payne, "The Govan Collieries, 1804-1805", Business History, III (1961), pp.75-96; A. Slaven, "Earnings and Productivity in the Scottish Coal-mining Industry during the Nineteenth Century: The Dixon Enterprises" in P.L. Payne, Studies in Scottish Business History, pp.217-49. William S. Dixon himself was described in The Bailie (28 November, 1877) as "a quiet, unassuming gentleman, who spends his time mainly between his house in London and his delightful estate at Belleisle, near Ayr", quoted by T.J. Byres, "Entrepreneurship in the Scottish Heavy Industries, 1879-1900" in P.L. Payne (ed.), Studies in Scottish Business History, p.270.

2. See also below, pp.89-90.

3. Quoted from the prospectus of Merry and Cunninghame by J.B. Jefferys, Business Organisation, pp.80-81, (the erroneous spelling of the names of both James Merry and Alexander Cunninghame has been corrected).

Forge Co., a few days later. The Glasgow Bessemer Steel Co. Ltd. took

over John M. Rowan's Atlas Works for a purchase price of £40,000, a

quarter of which was in the form of 1000 £10 shares.[1] But more important

were two new concerns: the Steel Company of Scotland, which was to dominate

the Scottish steel industry for more than two decades,[2] and the Eglinton

Chemical Co., whose works at Irvine were to become part of United Alkali

twenty years later. These latter companies, unlike earlier promotions,

represented a significant incursion of the limited company into Scotland's

economic development. Other new companies, while less powerful, helped

to strengthen the diversification of the nation's industrial base and to

demonstrate that the limited company was a viable organizational form for

a wide range of activities. Among the more interesting and successful were

Umpherston and Co., heavy engineers and machine tool makers; the great

North of Scotland Granite Co.; the Glasgow and West of Scotland Newspaper

Co., whose objective was the printing and publishing of newspapers

"advocating Conservative Principles", and whose first directors included

Sir William Stirling Maxwell, James Baird and Archibald Orr Ewing; the

North British Floor Cloth Co. of Kirkcaldy; the Aberdeen Jute Co., the

Guard Bridge Paper Co. whose original board was dominated by distillers,

members of the Haig family;[3] and the Dundee Aerated Water Manufacturing Co.

---

1. For the Atlas Works and Rowan's role in the establishment of the
   Scottish Steel Industry, see Payne, Colvilles ..., pp.22-5.

2. See I.F. Gibson, "The Establishment of the Scottish Steel Industry",
   Scottish Journal of Political Economy, V(1958), pp.22-39; Payne,
   Colvilles ..., pp.24-41, 59-66.

3. For Guard Bridge, see Lorna Weatherill, One Hundred Years of Paper-
   making: An Illustrated History of the Guardbridge Paper Company Ltd.,
   1873-1973 (Guardbridge, Fife: Guardbridge Paper Co. Ltd., 1974).

whose directorate included nine spirit dealers seeking, no doubt, either
to control a source of admixtures for their whisky or gin or to cover
themselves in the unlikely event of the success of the temperance movement
whose vigorous activities was about to give rise to a rash of tea and
coffee taverns, limited "public houses" where no alcohol was to be sold,[1]
and to numerous hydropathic establishments, whose menus, cynics observed,
were confined to "porridge and prayers".[2]

The incorporation of these companies, relatively modest in terms of
their aggregate demand for capital, did little to reduce the growing pressure
in Scotland for profitable outlets for savings.[3] Some relief was afforded
by the promotion of numerous substantial concerns whose principle objective
was to receive money on deposit and to make advances for the purchase of
heritable property,[4] but it was not enough. The Scots, not for the first

---

1. The distillers and spirit merchants need not have worried: few of the
   temperance establishments registered in the late 'seventies lasted more
   than a year or two.

2. W.H. Marwick, op.cit., p.421.

3. Some indication of which is provided by the massive increase in the
   total sum standing to the credit of depositors in the Savings Bank of
   Glasgow, in both the Ordinary and Investment Departments, from the late
   'nineties onward. Payne, "Savings Bank of Glasgow", pp.155, 170, 178.

4. Among them were The North British Property Investment Co., The Northern
   Heritable Securities Investment Co., The Aberdeen Heritable Securities
   Investment Co., The Glasgow Heritable Securities Co., The Scottish
   Provident Investment Co., The Edinburgh Heritable Security Co., The
   National Property Investment Co., The West of Scotland Lands and
   and Buildings Investment Co., The Scottish Heritages Co., and The
   Heritable Property Trust. Not without reason did Marwick, op.cit.,
   p.420, observe that "to a confusing degree almost every relevant
   combination of epithets was utilized in their nomenclature".

time, looked overseas.[1] Earlier ventures in North America and Australia
had been based on large co-partneries. One of the first limiteds was the
New Zealand and Australian Land Co.. Organized by James Morton, this
company was floated in 1866 with a nominal capital of £2 millions, of which
over £1 million had been called up by 1871, the majority of the shares being
held by the City of Glasgow Bank.[2] This was but the first of many such
joint stock ventures. By 1884, "a writer in Blackwood's Edinburgh Magazine
could comment that 'three-fourths of the foreign and colonial investment
companies are of Scottish origin. If not actually located in Scotland, they
have been hatched by Scotch-men, and work on Scottish models'".[3] Even before
the end of the 'sixties no less than a quarter of all the capital raised by
Scottish limiteds was destined for investment overseas (see Table 19). Some
companies were specifically concerned with the exploitation of mineral
resources. The Tharsis Sulphur and Copper Co. and Rio Tinto[4] sought to tap
the mineral wealth of Spain, the Patara Silver Lead Mining and Smelting Co.
that of Peru, and the Glasgow Port Washington Iron and Coal Co. that of Ohio.

---

1. For a succinct explanation of why "a case can be made for the selection
    of 1873 as the beginning date for the modern period of Scottish overseas
    investment", see W. Turrentine Jackson, op.cit., pp.8-11. Jackson's
    study is an indispensible guide to the subject of Scottish investment in
    the United States. A useful introduction to investment in Australia is
    provided by David S. Macmillan, "Scottish Enterprise in Australia, 1798-
    1879", in Payne (ed.), Studies in Scottish Business History, pp.319-44.

2. R.E. Tyson has spent many years in disentangling the affairs of the
    notorious City of Glasgow Bank whose fortunes were linked indissoluably
    with the New Zealand and Australia Land Co. It is to be hoped that his
    full findings will eventually be published. Meanwhile, see his essay
    "Scottish Investment in American Railways: the Case of the City of
    Glasgow Bank, 1856-1881" in Payne, Studies in Scottish Business History,
    pp.387-416. There is much of value in S.G. Checkland, Scottish Banking,
    pp.469-78. A useful article is that by R.N. Forbes, "Some Contemporary
    Reactions to a Banking Failure", Three Banks Review, Number 121 (March,
    1979), pp.42-57.

3. Macmillan, "Scottish Enterprise ...", p.341.

4. See S.G. Checkland, The Mines of Tharsis (London: Allen & Unwin, 1967).

Canadian copper was to be won by the Huntington Copper and Sulphur Co.,
the Consolidated Copper Co. of Canada and the Canadian Copper Pyrites and
Chemical Co.. Showing considerable discernment, the investing public was
not seduced by the impressive array of subscribers to the Articles of
Association, nor by the proposed directorate of Consolidated Copper, which
was abortive. After chequered careers, the other Canadian companies, both
of which were promoted by the Hon. Lucius S. Huntington, M.P., a Montreal
politician, were subsequently sold to the Canadian Copper and Sulphur Co.
Ltd..[1] The Harveyhill Copper Co., a lesser Canadian concern with a
nominal capital of but £95,000, was judicially wound up within five years
of its incorporation, its prospects having proved "entirely elusive",
mining had ceased, the banks had "entered into possession of the property
and advertised it for sale". The Secretary remarked to the Registrar that
he had failed even to induce a sufficient number of members to constitute
a quorum to attend the meeting called to authorize winding up the company.

Greater long-term success attended those who promoted and invested
in a number of companies whose principal objective was the manufacture of
jute and the establishment of coffee plantations in India.[2] But, infinitely
more important than these single-purpose ventures, were the investment trusts
which were to channel hundreds of thousands of pounds into American stock
market securities and real estate during subsequent decades. The earliest

---

1. Marwick, "The Limited Co....", p.421, and the company files (Huntington,
   BT2/408; Canadian Copper Pyrites, BT2/441).

2. For example, The East Bengal Co. and the Champdany Jute Co.. The
   former company returned £186.80 for every ordinary share of £100 when
   the firm went into voluntary liquidation in 1942. After a noteworthy
   career, the Scottish Indian Coffee Co. Ltd., dominated by Inverness
   interests, sold out to a syndicate in 1897.

of these peculiarly Scottish institutions were the Edinburgh-based Scottish-American Investment Co. and the Dundee-based Scottish American Investment Trust and the Oregon and Washington Trust Investment Co.. These three companies were incorporated in 1873. They were to be followed by many similar concerns, all of them modelled upon organizations pioneered by W.J. Menzies, W.S., of Edinburgh and Robert Fleming of Dundee.[1]

By the mid-'seventies, the limited company had secured a foothold in almost every branch of economic activity in Scotland. True, there were large areas in which earlier forms of business organizations remained supreme: in foodstuffs, clothing, the products of wood, stone and glass, in non-ferrous metals and major branches of machinery, but future trends were unmistakable. In 1873, the called-up capital of all Edinburgh registered companies exceeded £10 millions; within two decades this figure was to be increased four-fold, the greatest proportionate increase coming in domestic manufacturing and agricultural activities overseas. As Kerr has demonstrated, "the Prairie Cattle Co. Ltd. was the first large-scale joint stock venture by British capital in cattle ranching in Texas". Founded in Edinburgh in 1880, "two years after it began operations it paid a dividend of $19\frac{1}{2}$ per cent, followed by a payment to shareholders of almost 28 per cent in 1883. The Prairie experience set off the Scottish-American cattle craze".[2] Within five years, well over £2 million had been called up by the Prairie and those companies that followed its example: the Texas Land and Cattle Co., the Wyoming Cattle Ranch Co., the Western American

---

1. See, particularly, W. Turrentine Jackson, op.cit., and W.G. Kerr, op.cit..

2. W.G. Kerr, "Scottish Investment and Enterprise in Texas", in Payne (ed.), Studies in Scottish Business History, p.367.

Cattle Co., the Matador Land and Cattle Co., the Hansford Land and Cattle
Co., the Highland Mexican Land and Live Stock Co., the Montana Sheep and
Cattle Co., Chalk Buttes Ranch and Cattle Co., Park Red River Valley Land
Co., the Mapleton Farming Co., and Mitchell Innes Brothers Ltd.. Promoters
"with ranches in their pockets" flocked to Dundee, Edinburgh, Glasgow,
Aberdeen, Inverness and Greenock. Few went away completely empty-handed:
only the Deer Trail Land and Cattle Co. failed to float. The others, whose
directorates boasted such names as the Earl of Airlie, John Guthrie Smith,
Sheriff of Aberdeen and Kincardineshire, William Lawson, W.J. Menzies,
Thomas Nelson, the publisher, Sir George Warrender of Lochend, Robert
Fleming and Archibald Coats, all heavily involved in investment trusts, were
successfully started and for a few years, at least, lived up to the promises
so invitingly set forth in their prospectuses, though it would be interesting
to discover what Sir George Warrender, who was reported to be able to "snuff
out" unruly stockholders "in a very polite and decided way",[1] told the
meeting that voted to wind up the Western American Cattle Co. within a year
of its incorporation.

The cattle ranching craze was short-lived. It was over by 1886.
Yet so much excitement did it generate - and so well has it been documented[2] -
that there has been a tendency for it to overshadow more solid developments
elsewhere. In the six years (1880-1885) during which £2 million had been
poured into lands and cattle in the American West, the aggregate paid-up

1. Sir George Warrender's abilities were set down by John Clay, My Life
   on the Range (Chicago: Privately Printed, 1924), p.14, quoted by
   Jackman, op.cit., p.14.

2. A useful summary is provided by Richard Graham, "The Investment Boom
   in British-Texan Cattle Companies, 1880-1885", Business History Review,
   XXXIV (1960), pp.421-45.

capital in Scottish companies engaged in manufacturing had risen from
£4.6 million to £8.4 million and investments in public utilities had all
but doubled to £5.3 million. Steadily, and without fuss, capital in
Edinburgh-registered industrials had risen from 15.5 per cent of the whole
in 1866 to 31.4 per cent by the end of 1886. By the mid-'nineties, the
proportion was to exceed 40 per cent. Much of the capital was tightly held:
partnerships in many of the principle mining, iron and steel, shipbuilding
and engineering firms were being converted into private companies: so too
in brewing, where William Younger and William McEwan adopted the company
form,[1] as did J. & P. Coats, the Paisley cotton-thread manufacturers,
thereby boosting the capital invested in the manufacturing groups by a
massive £1 million.[2]

But the limited was spreading beyond these spectacular conversions,
overwhelmingly important though they were. As Jefferys has so clearly
shown, "for some 'new' and semi-new projects, the company rather than the
private partnership was /increasingly/ regarded as the most satisfactory
method of raising the capital needed".[3] Several foodstuffs came to be made
by limited concerns with initially modest capitals; many small chemical

---

1. Much valuable information on companies within the Scottish brewing
   industry and the capitals involved is to be found in Ian Donnachie,
   A History of the Brewing Industry in Scotland, pp.160-179. Donnachie's
   estimate (pp.162, 165) of the total capital of the industry in 1895
   at £5 million (of which £1.5 million was fixed and £3.5 million was
   trading capital) is particularly noteworthy.

2. J. & P. Coats adopted the company form somewhat tentatively. The
   first step, taken in 1884, was to convert the original partnership
   into an unlimited company in which nine members of the Coats family
   took all the shares. This company went into voluntary liquidation
   in order to transfer the business to a limited company in 1890. SRO,
   Dissolved Companies Register, BT2/1414 and M. Blair, The Paisley Thread
   Industry (Paisley: Alexander Gardner, 1907), pp.52-3.

3. J.B. Jefferys, Business Organization, p.127.

companies and machine shops, frequently established to exploit patents, were floated; a dozen or more companies were created to produce electrical machinery and apparatus; other limiteds made bicycles, photographic equipment and scientific instruments. Only clothing and apparel and carpets resisted the tide.

The limited form had quickly been adopted in shipping: no less than four of the eight Scottish companies formed in 1856 were engaged in coastal and ocean shipping and there followed a steady trickle of conversions and new projects, including the Albion Shipping Co., the Irrawady Flotilla and Burmese Steam Navigation Co.,[1] the State Line;[2] the British and African Steam Navigation Co., which went limited in 1883 after fourteen years of successful existence as a simple joint stock company, the Greenock Steamship Co., and the Aberdeen and Glasgow Steam Shipping Co., which in 1886 followed "the example of other companies" and successfully petitioned for a reduction of capital "due to the unprecendented fall in the value of shipping". Some part of this fall undoubtedly stemmed from

---

1. Formed within a few months of each other, these two prominent shipping lines originally had almost identical boards. The Albion's consisted of Peter Denny, James Galbraith, James Nicol Fleming, William Davie, Thomas Dunlop Findlay and Robert Henderson; the Irrawaddy's was the same, with the addition of John M'Ausland, Peter Denny's partner in William Denny & Brothers of Dumbarton.

2. The State Steamship Co., floated in 1872 with a nominal capital of £1 million, was abortive. Within a few weeks of incorporation it went into voluntary liquidation so that a new company, the State Line Steamship Co., could be registered with a nominal capital of £600,000 to take over the business. This company, too, soon got into difficulties and the line's seven steamships and the goodwill of the business were acquired in 1876 by a new company, the State Steamship Co. Ltd., for a purchase price of £225,000. (The called-up capital of the State Line Steamship Co. at the time of its dissolution stood at £403,024.) The nominal capital of the State Steamship Co., £300,000 at the outset, was reduced to £150,000 in 1887, and the called-up capital of £25,000, halved.

the contemporary mania in single-ship companies. Originated in Liverpool in 1878,[1] the incorporation of limited liability companies owning but one ship spread rapidly. This was partly a response to technological changes (iron-hulled ships with compound engines were more expensive than wooden sailing vessels, thus making the old 64th system unwieldy and inadequate) and partly a consequence of the desire to avoid or escape undue risk. As Jefferys explains: "the great advantage to ship owners of the limited liability system was that in the event of an accident involving a compensatory action by another ship owner, the amount that could be paid was limited. If the 'limited liability' ship had been responsible for the collision but in this collision it had been sunk, then the owners of the other vessel could get no compensation at all unless the limited ship in question was only one of a fleet of ships owned by the same company". This was why "the conversion of a line of steamers into so many 'single ship companies' became so common in the 'eighties",[2] and why the ownership of so many new vessels came to be organized in a similar manner.[3]

Between 1881 and mid-1895 no less than 251 single-ship companies were incorporated in Edinburgh. Their aggregate called-up capital had reached almost £3 million by the latter date (see Table 15), a figure which represented over 6 per cent of the capital invested in all Scottish companies

---

1. Shannon, "The Limited Companies", p.306.

2. Jefferys, Business Organization, p.70.

3. The advantages and drawbacks of the system of single-ship companies are clearly and comprehensively examined by James Mackenzie, "Ship Owning by Shares and by Single Ship Companies", Accountants' Magazine, Vol.II (1898), pp.100-111; see also R.S. Craig, "Some Aspects of Capital Formation in Shipping in the Age of Sail and Steam" (a paper for the Ealing Business History Seminar, May 1975), pp.10-18.

TABLE 15

SCOTTISH "SINGLE SHIP COMPANIES" NUMBER FORMED,
NUMBER IN EXISTENCE AND CAPITAL CALLED UP

	1881	1882	1883	1884	1885	1886	1887	1888
Number Formed	7	15	18	8	6	6	9	17
Number Dissolved	0	0	2	2	0	8	6	3
Number in Existence at Year End	7	22	38	44	50	48	51	65
Capital Called up at Year End (£1000's)	98.8	377.6	671.0	748.5	788.3	827.1	897.3	1,096
Average Capital per Company (£000's)	14.1	17.2	17.7	17.0	15.8	17.2	17.6	16.9
Proportion of Total Capital in Scottish Co's (%)	0.6	1.8	2.8	2.9	2.9	2.8	3.0	3.4

	1889	1890	1891	1892	1893	1894	1895*
Number Formed	22	18	27	29	26	32	11
Number Dissolved	5	6	3	9	14	9	7
Number in Existence at Year End	82	94	118	138	150	173	177
Capital Called up at Year End (£000's)	1,349.9	1,597.4	2,064.3	2,359.0	2,464.2	2,899.4	2,905.4
Average Capital per Company (£000's)	16.5	17.0	17.5	17.1	16.4	16.8	16.4
Proportion of Total Capital in Scottish Co's (%)	4.0	4.4	5.9	6.2	6.0	6.7	6.4

*The figures for 1895 are for only the first six months of the year

in the early 'nineties. Owned by an ever-changing kaleidoscope of shareholders among whom frequently figured one or more representatives of the
yards responsible for building the vessels, the majority of these ships were
managed by a relatively small group of partnerships. Among the more
prominent of these ship brokers were Wright and Breakenridge, James Little
and Co., Bell Brothers and M'Lelland, Maclay and M'Intyre, Thomson, Dickie
and Co. and J.D. and C.W. Clink, all of whom managed at least six vessels.
The greatest of the managing partnerships was Maclay and M'Intyre, whose
interests are shown in Table 16, but the others were hardly less powerful.
Ship-owning was still a preserve for gentlemen. The denomination of shares
was rarely less than £100 and they were taken up by leading industrialists
and financiers. Anxious, no doubt, to secure some leverage in the means
whereby many of their raw materials were conveyed to Scotland and their
finished products exported throughout the world, they were not averse to
a little potentially lucrative speculation. Besides, membership of a
single-ship company may have helped to cement connections. In the closing
years of the nineteenth century, ships were becoming highly complex,
dependent for their construction and fitting out on the assembly of an
ever-widening range of components, the acquisition of which was dependent
upon intricate credit relationships. It is difficult to imagine that no
commercial spin-off resulted from these associations of iron masters,
steel makers, marine engineers, ship builders, marine insurance brokers
and bank directors.

Everywhere it was the same. Because the most important companies
were mainly conversions, their direction and management - such was the
high proportion of the share capital allotted to the vendors - remained

TABLE 15

SINGLE-SHIP COMPANIES, INCORPORATED BETWEEN 1885 AND MID-1895, MANAGED BY JOSEPH P. MACLAY & THOMAS W. M'INTYRE, GLASGOW

Reg. No. BT2/	Name of Steamship Company	Date of Incorporation	Nominal Capital (£s)	Maximum Called-up Capital (£s)	Date of Dissolution[1]	Notable Subscribers and Shareholders[2]	Vessel Built (B) or Purchased	Management Salary (£s Per Annum)	Remuneration Share of Net Profits
1456	Gordon	April 1885	21,000	16,100	June 1919	James S.Napier, Iron Merchant; John Stephen, Shipbuilder	B: Alex Stephen & Co.	n.d.	n.d.
1677	Victoria	October 1887	20,000	16,600	October 1917	J.B.Smith, Iron Founder; John Stephen	B: Alex Stephen & Co.	n.d.	n.d.
1720	Domira	March 1888	20,000	19,000	June 1919	James Napier, Iron Merchant; James Stevenson, Merchant	B: Alex Stephen & Co.	n.d.	n.d.
1859	Mangara	June 1889	20,500	20,000	October 1916	W.Macadam Smith, Iron Founder; John Stephen	B: Alex Stephen & Co.	200	10%
1861	Nyassa	June 1889	25,500	22,500	November 1914	W.Macadam Smith; John Stephen; British Investment Trust	B: Alex Stephen & Co.	200	10%
1883	Samara	July 1889	20,500	20,000	October 1916	W.Macadam Smith; James McMurray, Paper Maker	B: Mackie & Thomson	200	10%
2117	Mereddio[3]	February 1891	14,720	14,720	June 1919	James Napier; James R. Sloan, Manufacturer; W.Wilson, Iron Merchant	Purchased	200	10%
2118	Meraggio[4]	February 1891	9,280	9,280	June 1914	James Napier; George G. Napier, Iron Merchant; James R.Sloan; W.Wilson	Purchased	200	10%
2119	Mersario[5]	February 1891	16,960	16,960	October 1915	James Napier; George G. Napier; James R.Sloan; W.Wilson	Purchased	200	10%
2120	Merannio[6]	February 1891	8,640	8,640	February 1917	James Napier; George G. Napier; James R.Sloan; W.Wilson	Purchased	150	10%
2312	Uganda	April 1892	27,000	22,000	October 1916	James S. Napier; John Stephen	B: Alex Stephen & Co.	200	10%

TABLE 16 (continued)

Reg. No. BT2/	Name of Steamship Company	Date of Incorporation	Nominal Capital (£s)	Maximum Called-up Capital (£s)	Date of Dissolution[1]	Notable Subscribers and Shareholders[2]	Vessel Built (B) or Purchased	Management Salary (£s Per Annum)	Remuneration Share of Net Profits
2397	Cartagena[7]	November 1892	14,000	14,000	April 1894	James McMurray	Purchased	200	10%
2487	Rowena (of Glasgow)[8]	April 1893	9,600	–	February 1894		Purchased	200	10%
2488	Ivanhoe[9]	April 1893	7,040	7,040	October 1916	J. Adam, Marine Insurance Broker	Purchased	175	5%
2489	Peveril[10]	April 1893	7,040	7,040	October 1916	J. Adam; Maj. J. Finlaw, "Gentleman", Surrey	Purchased	175	5%
2490	Inverleith[11]	April 1893	8,000	8,000	October 1902			150	10%
2491	Behera[12]	April 1893	6,400	6,400	November 1914	Henry Birkmyre, Rope Maker, Pt. Glasgow	Purchased	150	10%
2501	Craigendoran[13]	May 1893	9,600	9,600	October 1917	John Ferguson, Shipbuilder, London	Purchased	150	10%
2503	Edward Williams[14]	May 1893	3,840	3,780	January 1899	Robb, Moore & Co., Merchants & Shipowners, Glasgow	Purchased	150	10%
2639	Jeanara	March 1893	32,000	25,000	October 1916	John Stephen; Latterly British Steamship Investment Trust	B: Alex Stephen & Co.	250	10%
2640	Janeta	March 1893	32,000	25,000	October 1924	John Stephen, Fred W. Harris & James Dixon, Shipowners, London	B: Alex Stephen & Co.	250	10%
2641	Rutherglen	March 1893	30,000	27,400	June 1919	James McMurray; W. Macadam Smith; James Napier	n.d.	200	10%
2642	Everilda	March 1893	8,000	6,665	June 1919	S.S. Edward Williams & Co. Ltd.; W. Macadam Smith, James Napier	n.d.	200	10%

TABLE 16 (continued)

Reg. No. BT2/	Name of Steamship Company	Date of Incorporation	Nominal Capital (£s)	Maximum Called-up Capital (£s)	Date of Dissolution[1]	Notable Subscribers and Shareholders[2]	Vessel Built (B) or Purchased	Management Salary (£s Per Annum)	Remuneration Share of Net Profits
2643	Marthara	March 1893	25,000	20,000	October 1919	James Stevenson; John Stephen; James McMurray	n.d.	200	10%
2644	Madura	March 1893	25,000	800	November 1900	J.& P.Henderson & Co., Shipbuilders, Partick	B: J.& P. Henderson	200	10%
2760	Alaska	October 1894	10,000	6,700	November 1919	James Napier; W.P.Maclay, Merchant	n.d.	200	10%
2930	Oceana	June 1895	32,000	21,000	June 1919	W.Macadam Smith	B: Alex Stephen & Co.	250	10%
2931	Magdala[15]	June 1895	32,000	20,500	March 1953	W.Macadam Smith	B: Alex Stephen & Co.	250	10%

[1]During the first six months of 1908, all the single-ship companies being managed by Maclay & M'Intyre, following alterations to their Articles of Association, were converted into private companies under the Act of 1907.

[2]In addition to Maclay & M'Intyre.

[3]File contains 18 separate agreements for the transfer of 29/64's in the vessel; Maclay & M'intyre already held 18/64's.

[4]Twenty-one separate agreements for transfer of 29/64's in the vessel. Maclay & M'Intyre already held 13/64's.

[5]Nineteen separate agreements for transfer of 37/64's; Maclay & M'Intyre already held 9/64's.

[6]Nineteen separate agreements for transfer of 33/64's in the vessel; Maclay & M'Intyre already held 9/64's.

[7]James McMurray sold the vessel to the Company for L14,000.

[8]Abortive: ship wrecked before transfer to Company.

[9]Twenty-three separate agreements for transfer of 58/64's in the vessel; Maclay & M'Intyre already held 6/64's.

[10]Nineteen separate agreements for transfer of 55/64's in vessel; Maclay & M'Intyre already held 8/64's.

[11]Twenty-five separate agreements for transfer of 42/64's in vessel; Maclay & M'Intyre already held 20/64's.

[12]Nineteen separate agreements for transfer of 51/64's in vessel; Maclay & M'Intyre already held 12/64's.

[13]Twenty-four separate agreements for transfer of 54/64's in vessel; Maclay & M'Intyre already held 10/64's.

[14]Twenty-nine separate agreements for transfer of 58/64's in vessel; Maclay & M'Intyre already held 5/64's.

[15]By the time of the dissolution of this company, by which time it had disposed of the Magdala and assumed ownership of the S.S. Masunda, each £100 share had returned £1,641 to the owners.

in the hands of those who had controlled the former partnerships.[1]
Nevertheless, the greater flexibility and infinitely greater security of
the limited liability form of business organization was instrumental in
consolidating, enhancing and diversifying the power of a relatively small
group of men to whom W.H. Marwick first drew attention over forty years
ago.[2] Scotland had its own economic aristocracy, and if some of its
members, like Sir Charles Tennant, went on "to greater things" in the
metropolis and in international big business,[3] there were others
scrambling to take their places. The catholicity of some directors and
major shareholders was remarkable: their names are to be found in the
company files of leading concerns in mining, the heavy industries, transport,
banking, property and real estate and many branches of overseas enterprise.
Many of them, men such as Thomas Aitken of Nivingston, Henry Birkmyre,
Archibald and Thomas Coats, Sir James King of Campsie, Peter McLagan of
Pumpherston, James Morton, James S. Napier and Thomas Reid, deserve
further study. Here it is sufficient to note the interlocking of interests
that was facilitated (not created, for such a phenomenon dates back to
the days of the partnership) by the advent of the limited company which
had come to dominate almost every branch of Scotland's economy by the end

1. Jefferys, Business Organisation, pp.116-7, emphasizes this point; as
   does Essex-Crosby: "The effective control in individual companies was
   concentrated in family holdings in almost all groups (other than
   banking and insurance) engaged in home enterprise, and the 'ideal'
   conception of the joint stock company as an organisation embodying
   diffused ownership and democratic control was imperfectly realised".
   Essex-Crosby, op.cit., p.210.

2. Marwick, "The Limited Company", pp.428-9.

3. This point has been made elsewhere, see Payne, "Industrial Entrepreneurship", pp.674-5, note 131.

of the nineteenth century.[1]

IV

THE CAPITAL OF THE EARLY SCOTTISH
JOINT STOCK COMPANIES

Forty years after the passage of the Act of 1856 the total nominal
capital of the surviving non-railway Edinburgh-registered joint stock
companies exceeded £110 million,[2] of which about half had been called up.[3]
Even the nominal capital of those companies subsequently dissolved stood
at over £91 million at the end of 1894 (the last year for which complete
data have been abstracted from the files). Of this, £43.5 million, or
47.8 per cent, had been called up (Table 12).

As has already been suggested,[4] perhaps the greatest value of the
figures showing the aggregate nominal capital of the companies incorporated

---

1. The entire question of incorporate connections in the Scottish economy
   since the early years of the twentieth century is currently being
   examined by John Scott and Michael Hughes. See their "Ownership and
   Control in a Satellite Economy: A Discussion from Scottish Data",
   Sociology, Vol.X, No.1 (January 1976), pp.21-41; "Patterns of Ownership in Top Scottish Companies" (with John Mackenzie), Scottish
   Journal of Sociology, Vol.1, No.1 (November 1976), pp.15-27; The
   Anatomy of Scottish Capital, forthcoming (London: Croom Helm, 1980),
   especially chapters 2 and 3. I am grateful to Dr. Scott for permitting
   me to read these chapters prior to publication.

2. This figure has been estimated on the basis of the known nominal
   capital of the companies in existence at the end of year 1894 which
   were subsequently dissolved to which has been added an estimate of
   the nominal capital of the companies formed in 1895 plus an estimate
   of the nominal capital of those companies formed between 1856 and 1895
   that were still in existence in 1970.

3. The called up capital represents the amount subscribed by the public
   in calls plus the amount considered as paid up on vendors' and other
   shares.

4. See above, p.22.

in each year (Table 17) is that they provide some indication of business optimism, but not too much significance should be attached to the magnitudes of the movements. Other factors were involved. For example, all the major Scottish banks adopted limited liability after the failure of the City of Glasgow Bank in 1878. The fact that the unfortunate stockholders of this unlimited bank had had to pay about £2,750 on each £100 share which they held at the time of the crash (i.e. if they remained solvent throughout the entire period during which calls were being made upon them) was the strongest inducement to both bank shareholders and the general public to accept the basic principle of limited liability in banking, hitherto regarded as a sign of insecurity.[1] Thus, the massive increase in the total nominal capital of the Scottish companies that occurred in the early 'eighties was largely due to the incorporation of the banks.

The National Bank of Scotland and the Union Bank of Scotland (both of which were subsequently involved in mergers and thus dissolved in their original form, thereby appearing in Table 17) had each a nominal capital of £5 million, and between them they contributed a large proportion of the total nominal capital of all the 104 companies incorporated in 1882.[2]

---

1. Jefferys, Business Organization, pp.101-2. For a detailed study of the causes and consequences of the failure of the City of Glasgow Bank, we must await the forthcoming study by R.E. Tyson; meanwhile, an excellent summary is provided by S.G. Checkland, Scottish Banking, pp.469-81.

2. The files of the Scottish banks are curiously incomplete. Only a few S.C.A.S. returns are contained therein and the other data are inexplicably fragmentary. It is worth noting that the Commercial Bank of Scotland and the Clydesdale Bank were also incorporated in 1882.

TABLE 14

THE NOMINAL CAPITAL OF SCOTTISH COMPANIES INCORPORATED IN EACH YEAR, 1856-1895 (ALL OF WHICH HAD BEEN DISSOLVED BY 1975)

Year	Number of Companies Formed	Nominal Capital (£s)	
		Total	Average
1856	7	554,500	79,214
1857	22	1,739,130	79,051
1858	14	156,450	11,175
1859	5	35,850	7,170
1860	13	94,950	7,304
1861	22	182,720	8,305
1862	33	5,397,500	163,561
1863	28	1,175,900	41,996
1864	27	2,985,898	110,588
1865	36	2,782,810	77,300
1866	36	4,081,020	113,362
1867	17	611,400	35,965
1868	25	827,700	33,108
1869	17	836,250	49,191
1870	17	475,850	27,991
1871	43	1,440,600	33,502
1872	78	7,191,920	92,204
1873	58	4,800,300	82,764
1874	59	5,081,250	86,123
1875	45	4,329,000	96,200
1876	60	3,970,262	66,171
1877	78	5,909,900	76,806
1878	56	2,300,900	41,088
1879	52	2,387,102	45,906
1880	66	6,114,240	92,640
1881	71	15,676,250	220,792
1882	104	17,541,110	168,665
1883	105	7,109,980	67,714
1884	101	10,839,820	107,325
1885	72	4,393,084	61,015
1886	90	8,724,926	96,944
1887	82	5,446,350	66,419
1888	109	7,380,954	67,715
1889	122	4,640,924	38,040
1890	124	6,175,190	49,800
1891	135	3,742,295	27,721
1892	148	5,129,169	34,657
1893	169	7,268,318	43,008
1894	180	4,463,920	24,800
1895[*]	223	8,957,910	40,170

[*]Estimated

This, however, is anomalous. In general, the relative magnitudes of the annual nominal figures afford some insight into general business confidence. Furthermore, after 1862 the average nominal capital per company formed at or near upper turning points of the cycle is usually higher than that of companies formed at or near the lower turning points.

Much more important than the figures for nominal capital are those for called-up capital. For Scottish companies dissolved before 1970, the total called-up capital of all those save domestic **railways** in existence at the end of each year 1856-1894 is given in Table 18, together with an estimate (almost certainly on the low side) of the called-up capital of all Scottish non-railway companies. After 1858 it will be observed that with the exception of the years 1877-79 and 1891, the figures show a rapid rate of increase (see Chart 6), though some falling off occurred around the mid-'eighties. This increase is largely a function of the formation of new companies, since the average called-up capital per company remained remarkably stable after 1862 (Table 12), fluctuating about a mean of £33,500, the figure for 1870. It would appear, if the official figures are reliable, that the average Scottish company, at first somewhat larger, was subsequently smaller than those registered in London. In 1887 the Registrar reported to the Select Committee on the Companies' Acts of 1862 and 1867 that about 7000 going concerns had an average paid-up capital of about £45,000; the Parliamentary return of 1883 gives an average of £53,000, whence it increased to a maximum of £64,000 in 1892, steadily to decline to £40,000 by 1913.[1]

---

1. Macgregor, "Joint Stock Companies", pp.501-2.

£s Million

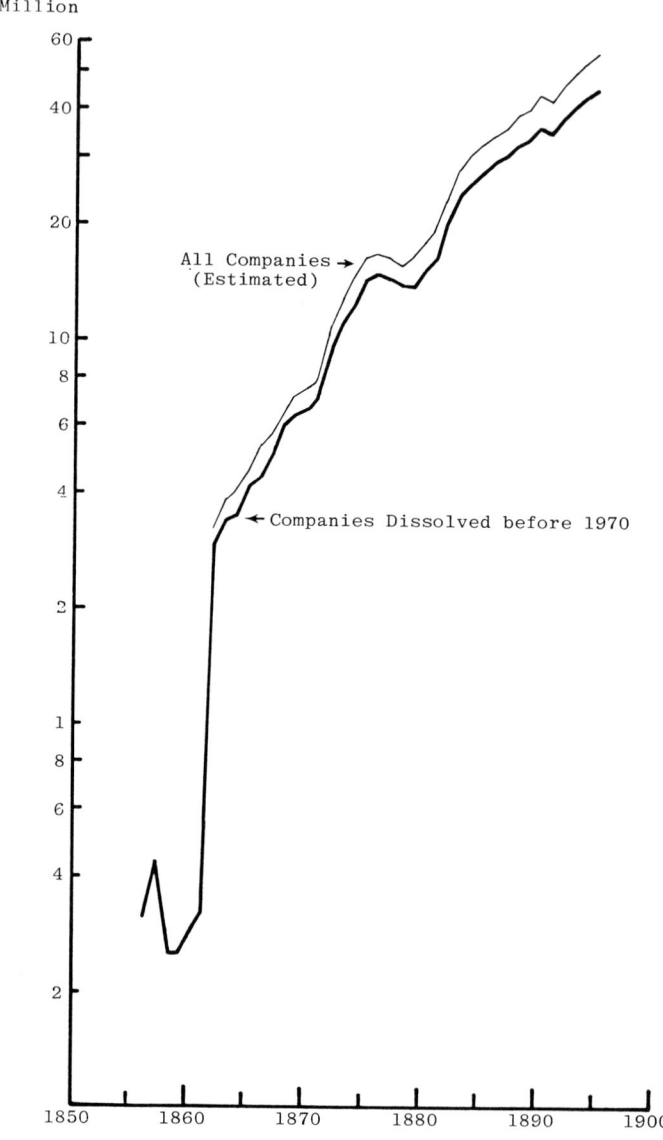

CHART 6:   Scottish Joint Stock Companies:
Capital Raised, 1856-1895
(£s Million)

- 78 -

In the absence of specific and comprehensive information on the composition of the surviving London-registered companies, any explanation of the lower average paid-up capital of the Scottish firms must be conjectural. It is possible that the difference resides in the greater proportion of Scottish companies engaged in branches of manufacturing compared with the English sample, swollen as it was with a disproportionate number of large banking and overseas ventures; or the explanation may lie in the higher proportion of Scottish firms that approached the form of private companies, legally unrecognised until 1907. Certainly, the average nominal capital of "private companies" was much lower than that of the public companies listed in Burdett's Official Intelligence and which constitute the basis of Jefferys' calculations.[1]

Whatever the reason for the differences in called-up capital, to have over £50 million invested in the shares of limited companies by the early 'nineties in addition to some £100 million in domestic railway companies[2] represented no mean performance by the Scottish economy.[3] Of this sum of £50 million,[4] if the companies subsequently dissolved are representative,

1. Ibid., p.503, c.f. Jefferys, Business Organization, pp.75-6, 130-31, and Appendix E, pp.458-60.

2. G.R. Hawke and M.C. Reed, "Railway Capital in the United Kingdom in the Nineteenth Century", Economic History Review, XXII (1969), p.272. More precisely the annual figures (in millions of £s) for the early 1890's, 95.7; 1891, 97.3; 1892, 99.6; 1893, 102.3; 1894, 104.2; 1895, 106.2.

3. It may be objected that a significant proportion of this capital probably came from south of the border. This is agreed (though cursory glances at the shareholders' lists of the companies considered in this paper give an overwhelming impression of local recruitment of capital), but it was almost certainly more than offset by investments by Scots in London-registered companies.

4. The economic significance of this figure is discussed more fully below, pp.93-94.

over 40 per cent was in manufacturing activity, nearly 20 per cent in public
utilities (broadly defined to include shipping; refer to Appendix Table 1),
14 per cent in mining and quarrying, 9 per cent in finance and insurance
and 8 per cent in agriculture, forestry and fishing. It was not always so
(see Table 18). During the first ten to fifteen years following the Act
of 1856, the leading industrial groups appear almost to jostle for first
place. The initial importance of public utilities swiftly gave way to
mining and quarrying which, in the early 'sixties, was overwhelmed (and
the word is carefully chosen) by Finance and Insurance. Thereafter,
relatively short-lived bursts of interest in one or other form of economic
activity (for example, in iron, steel and coal in the early 'seventies,
in banks in 1882, in overseas land companies in the period 1882-85) are
reflected in the annual data, but the relative movements are slower and
more sustained. In no group is this more so than in manufacturing, whose
share of total called-up capital moved almost relentlessly upward from
3 per cent in 1862/63, to 15 per cent in 1870, thence to 30 per cent in
1880 and, after slipping somewhat with the banking and overseas flotations
of the early 'eighties and the single-ship mania, to 40 per cent in the
mid-'nineties.

Moreover, most of this investment in manufacturing was located in
Scotland. Of the £19.33 million called up by Scottish manufacturing
companies in 1895, only £1.31 million (or 6.8 per cent) was directed
overseas (Tables 18 and 19). This is in marked contrast with the
Agriculture, Forestry and Fishing group in which, since the early
'eighties, over 90 per cent of the capital raised was for foreign and
colonial enterprise. Perhaps more remarkable than the home/overseas

ratios in each major industrial group, was the high proportion of the total capital raised that was destined for investment overseas. In only one year (1877) between 1868 and 1895 did this figure fall below 20 per cent. Indeed, it was rarely less than 25 per cent, reaching a high of 34.8 per cent in 1883 and hovering around a third of the total capital called up by Scottish companies throughout the latter part of the 'eighties.[1]

The period with which this paper is primarily concerned is insufficiently long and the focus of interest - the Scottish incorporated company - too narrow to draw any firm conclusions from the data that might shed light on the relative significance of "push versus pull" factors in determining Scottish overseas investment.[2] It may simply be observed that in supporting overseas ventures by Edinburgh-registered companies, Scottish investors seem to have been responding to the possibility of obtaining higher yields than were available in most branches of domestic economic activity (how else can the evidence of the prospectuses and newspaper "puffs" be interpreted?)[3] coupled with a

---

1. It is important to put the figures set out in Table 16 into perspective. Overseas investment by Edinburgh-registered joint stock companies may have constituted less than 10 per cent of total Scottish foreign investment in the 'eighties and, possibly, an even smaller proportion later in the century. The precise measurement of the volume of Scottish capital exports is, at present, impossible: a careful estimate gives £150 million for 1885 and £300 million in 1900. See S.G.E. Lythe and John Butt, An Economic History of Scotland, 1100-1939 (Glasgow & London: Blackie, 1975), p.236.

2. I find myself in greatest sympathy with the ideas put forward by Michael Edelstein, "The Determinants of U.K. Investment Abroad, 1870-1913: The U.S. Case", Journal of Economic History, XXXIV (1974), pp.980-1007.

3. On the whole question of financial news in the lay and specialist press, see N. Greiser, The British Investor and His Sources of Information (University of London: unpublished M.Sc. (Econ.) thesis, 1940).

relative dearth of <u>local</u> investment opportunities[1] until the capital needs
of the many great "conversions" that increasingly took place throughout the
second half of the nineteenth century outran both internally generated
profits and the resources of the vendors and the trusts that they established
for their kinfolk. Until this took place the great majority of the early
large firms were able to retain their "private" characteristics and refrain
from any appeal to a wider public; until, that is, the very eve of the First
World War, if not later.[2] This is not to say that the outsider was kept
at bay in every case. From the 'seventies onwards investment opportunities
increased with the flotation and growth of genuinely public companies with
heavy capital requirements; it was simply that they were insufficient to
absorb the available savings being generated by the Scottish economy.

There was too a pronounced speculative element in the outflow of
capital via the Scottish company. Archibald Coats, with the solid assets
of the family thread-making company behind him, appears always to have
been ready to venture considerable sums in schemes that strain credulity,
and even for those of lesser wealth, the lure of gold remained irresistible
throughout the century, whether it was to be found in the English West
Country, Wales or the uttermost parts of the globe. Scottish investors
may have purchased relatively safe and high-yielding foreign and colonial
bond issues with the rest: the overseas companies that they themselves

---

1. As a writer in Blackwood's <u>Edinburgh Magazine</u> observed in 1884: "The
    continuous and increasing efflux of capital abroad ... must sooner or
    later tell on the domestic supply. It is justified on the plea that
    money is a drug at home, and warnings like the present one met with
    a defiant retort - 'What home investments can you offer in their
    place?'." (Vol.136, 1884, p.476).

2. A number of examples are provided in the author's study of <u>Colvilles
    and the Scottish Steel Industry</u>, <u>passim.</u>

promoted and supported generally constituted far more of a flutter.[1]

Jefferys has drawn attention to the fact that during the period 1885-1914, "existing companies in each year tended to become more and more important as the channel for the savings of the investing classes as compared with new companies in that year". His argument is based upon figures drawn from the Annual Returns of Joint Stock Companies and the Annual Winding Up Reports. These show that "from 1892 to 1900 the capital issues in each year by new companies were greater than those of existing companies. For the period 1901 to 1914 the capital issues of existing companies in each year was very much greater than the issues of new companies, from 1910 onwards being almost seven times as great".[2] Table 20 provides similar data for the dissolved Scottish companies for the period 1856-1895. It will be observed that even within a decade or two of the Act of 1856, occasionally there were years (e.g. 1867) in which existing ("old") companies were calling up amounts of capital larger than newly incorporated companies, and an even greater number of years in which capital called up by "old" companies more than compensated for the share capital "lost" in liquidations (between 1856 and 1894 this occurred fifteen times). What is interesting is that whereas the capital

---

1. To a special meeting of shareholders, held in October 1883, of The Mysore Gold Mining Company (formed in 1879), Sir Charles Tennant said flatly: 'Gold Mining is a lottery'." Checkland, Tharsis, p.158. Indeed, as Clark C. Spence has shown, most of those putting their money into American mining activities were prepared to recognize that they were participating in a wager. Clark C. Spence, British Investments and the American Mining Frontier (Ithaca, New York: Cornell University Press, 1958), p.231.

2. Jefferys, Business Organization, pp.147-51, Appendix B, pp.452-53.

called up by "new" companies was frequently dominated by the amounts considered as paid up on vendors' and other shares,[1] the capital raised by existing companies appears to have represented amounts subscribed by the public. Moreover, these figures, presented in the last column of Table 20, provide a much better indication of purposeful capital investment (since a proportion of the sums raised were frequently for new capital formation[2]) than those in the second column, which in many years owe their magnitude to what were, in effect, transfer payments.[3]

Be that as it may, the aggregate figures for the entire period show that the dissolved Scottish companies raised at least £82-83 million in share capital in the forty years following the Act of 1856, about two-thirds of it in the calendar year in which incorporation took place. Of this sum £32.6 million (or 40 per cent) had been "lost" in liquidations by the summer of 1895 and about £3.2 million (or 4 per cent) in the writing down of capital.[4] But whereas the word "lost" may legitimately be used

---

1. The early company files do not provide data sufficiently comprehensive to measure this dominance.

2. The major obvious exceptions to this were in the fairly rare instances in which the board of an ailing company would call up capital in a desperate and invariably vain attempt to save the company from bankruptcy. In such cases, the paid-up capital suddenly rose (though not dramatically, since most shareholders tended to be wary in these circumstances) towards the very end of a sick company's life, only to be lost in the ensuing liquidation.

3. This important issue is discussed later, see below, pp. 89-93.

4. The figures in Col. 4, Table 20, "Capital raised by existing companies" are net of capital written down. Sometimes, as in the early 'nineties, this amount (plus the sums returned to the shareholders as being "in excess of the wants of the company") exceeded the capital raised by existing companies. The writing down of share capital and the return of capital to shareholders was largely confined to overseas ventures (mainly cattle and land companies) and shipping companies. A careful estimate indicates that the total amount so lost between 1876 and 1895 was about £3.2 million. Large sums were repaid to shareholders by several overseas ventures as a preparatory step to voluntary liquidation.

SHARE CAPITAL PAID UP BY SCOTTISH COMPANIES (ALL SUBSEQUENTLY DISSOLVED)
AND SHARE CAPITAL "LOST" BY LIQUIDATIONS, ANNUALLY, 1856 - MID-1895.

Year	Net Addition To Called-Up Capital During Year (£s)	Capital Called Up By Companies Incorporated During Year (£s)	Capital "Lost" By Liquidations During Year (£s)	Capital Raised By Existing ("Old") Companies During Year (£s)
1856	321,410	321,410	-	-
1857	135,219	135,148	-	71
1858	- 205,829	124,066	453,030	123,135
1859	6,168	6,862	204	490
1860	37,637	34,981	3,061	5,717
1861	35,501	58,235	32,244	9,510
1862	2,635,940	2,631,120	8,813	13,633
1863	479,472	481,094	37,392	35,770
1864	170,599	367,966	315,411	118,044
1865	627,220	666,822	30,506	- 9,096
1866	595,935	357,427	80,208	318,716
1867	273,564	54,296	42,053	261,321
1868	995,389	207,143	216,095	1,004,341
1869	417,893	230,849	175,359	362,403
1870	210,205	147,716	73,105	135,594
1871	494,836	325,719	93,485	262,602
1872	2,222,674	1,926,199	191,345	487,820
1873	1,923,435	1,338,059	102,807	688,183
1874	1,442,793	416,882	234,264	1,260,175
1875	1,969,672	824,562	849,977	1,995,087
1876	226,818	862,754	426,385	- 209,551
1877	288,962	1,059,424	2,810,439	1,462,053
1878	- 643,930	676,261	1,937,615	617,424
1879	- 126,446	439,212	1,009,094	443,436
1880	1,321,796	1,660,711	715,431	376,516
1881	1,362,578	1,910,377	1,083,934	536,135
1882	3,975,310	4,587,394	2,111,261	1,499,177
1883	3,417,813	2,726,002	1,709,595	2,401,406
1884	1,948,958	3,160,691	1,571,129	359,396
1885	1,619,008	1,396,403	1,299,513	1,522,118
1886	1,580,465	2,160,053	1,201,119	621,531
1887	870,688	1,411,478	729,291	188,501
1888	2,420,237	2,693,629	1,373,884	1,100,492
1889	952,874	1,978,117	1,651,711	626,468
1890	2,674,570	3,458,073	2,360,755	1,577,252
1891	- 1,371,636	1,731,829	2,007,531	- 1,095,934
1892	3,458,299	2,995,438	984,697	1,447,558
1893	2,681,004	4,951,961	2,164,724	- 106,233
1894	2,674,421	2,776,652	1,443,164	1,340,933
1895 *	2,058,991	2,323,984	1,022,406	757,413
1856 - Mid-1895	45,602,589	55,616,999	32,553,037	22,538,627

* June 1895

to describe the amount of capital written down by existing companies, it is too strong a word to employ in connection with the share capital removed from the Register in liquidations. For example, it is manifestly incorrect to say that the capital of companies that were sold, amalgamated or reconstructed (Mode of Dissolution Type 2) was lost. What, then, was the true loss involved? The information that might have enabled a proper calculation of this figure appears in the company files sparsely and in a most erratic and fragmentary manner. Therefore, it is possible only to estimate the size of the annual losses brought about by company failure.

The following assumptions, based on empirical (if spotty) evidence in each category, have been made in the composition of such estimates:

(i)   The firms that disappeared in their original form each year possessed a paid-up capital equal to the estimated average of the companies in existence during the year in which they were removed from the Register (the only exceptions being that it is assumed that abortive companies had, at the time of their dissolution or disappearance, raised only 10 per cent of this average figure);

(ii) of the sum raised by abortives, 50 per cent was completely lost to the shareholders;

(iii) companies sold, amalgamated or reconstructed, lost 20 per cent of their share capital;

(iv) insolvent firms (Mode of Dissolution Type 3) lost 90 per cent of their share capital;

(v)   firms wound up voluntarily (Mode of Dissolution Type 4) lost 50 per cent of their share capital;

(vi) firms that dissolved in disregard of legal forms (Mode of Dissolution Type 5), in short, those that simply

withered away, lost 100 per cent of their share capital;

(vii) between 1876 and 1895 the sum of £3.2 million was lost

to shareholders in the writing down of capital, most of

it in the second half of the period.

On the basis of these assumptions, the true annual percentage loss to

the shareholders in Scottish companies may be expressed thus:

$$c = \frac{\left(\Sigma_{i=1}^{5} a_i n_i\right) k + w}{nk}$$

where

c = the capital loss expressed as a proportion of the estimated

called-up capital of all Scottish companies at the end of

each year (i.e. the capital at risk) (see Table 12);

i = the modes of dissolution, characterized as types 1-5 (see

above, p.8, and Table 4);

a_i = the percentage loss of capital for each type of dissolution

as set forth above;

k = the estimated average called-up capital per company;

w = the estimated amount lost by the writing down of capital;

and n = the total number of Scottish companies in existence.

Although this formula produced some anomalies, especially in the early

years when the total number of cases was small and their distribution among

the various modes of dissolution was unrepresentative, much more plausible

results were produced for the last twenty-five years of the period (see

Table 21). If the fact that the formula occasionally produced patently

TABLE 21

ESTIMATED ANNUAL TRUE LOSS ON THE PAID-UP CAPITAL OF SCOTTISH NONRAILWAY COMPANIES, 1870-1894
(in Thousands of £s)

Year	(1) (Estimated) Average Called-up Capital for Company	(2)-(6) Estimated True Loss by Liquidation, by Mode of Dissolution (No. of cases x assumed percentage loss)					(7) Total of Cols. (2)-(6) [1]	(8) Estimated Additional Loss by writing down Capital [2]	(9) Total Estimated True Loss	(10) Called-up Capital at risk	(11) Col. (8) / Col. (9) [3]
		(1) 5%	(3) 20%	(4) 90%	(5) 50%	(6) 100%					
1870	33.5	--	6.7	--	67.0	33.5	107.2*	--	107.2	7,507.1	1.4
1871	30.5	6.1	6.1	--	61.0	--	73.2	--	73.2	7,810.8	0.9
1872	31.8	9.5	--	28.6	159.0	31.8	228.9*	--	228.9	10,440.6	2.2
1873	33.1	8.3	6.6	59.6	66.2	33.1	173.8*	--	173.8	12,601.0	1.4
1874	34.6	15.6	6.9	31.1	173.0	--	226.6	--	226.6	14,725.7	1.5
1875	37.0	5.6	44.4	166.5	259.0	37.0	512.5	--	512.5	16,416.6	3.1
1876	34.9	8.7	27.9	94.2	226.9	69.8	427.5*	313.7	741.2	16,972.2	4.4
1877	31.3	14.1	68.9	112.7	313.0	93.9	602.6	82.4	685.0	16,478.6	4.2
1878	28.6	11.4	17.2	154.4	257.4	143.0	583.4	81.8	665.2	15,772.6	4.2
1879	28.8	13.0	11.5	285.1	158.4	201.6	669.6	82.9	752.5	16,576.0	4.5
1880	29.2	5.8	46.7	262.8	102.2	175.2	592.7	44.5	637.2	17,815.8	3.6
1881	29.5	5.9	17.7	371.7	103.3	88.5	587.1	48.3	635.4	19,321.9	3.3
1882	32.9	14.8	52.6	296.1	148.1	98.7	610.3	60.1	670.4	24,036.6	2.8
1883	35.6	16.0	78.3	448.6	338.2	213.6	1,094.7	70.1	1,164.8	28,052.3	4.2
1884	35.4	15.9	49.6	414.2	247.8	35.4	762.9	152.1	915.0	30,414.7	3.0
1885	36.6	9.2	51.2	395.3	274.5	256.2	986.4	162.5	1,148.9	32,501.7	3.5
1886	36.9	18.5	66.4	631.0	276.8	110.7	1,103.4	170.8	1,274.2	34,163.8	3.7
1887	37.1	13.0	37.1	333.9	519.4	259.7	1,163.1*	89.5	1,252.6	35,797.8	3.5
1888	37.5	16.9	60.0	573.8	450.0	112.5	1,213.2	96.6	1,309.8	38,623.9	3.4
1889	36.3	14.5	72.6	588.1	326.7	363.0	1,364.9	100.0	1,464.9	39,989.1	3.7
1890	36.1	5.4	108.3	422.4	451.3	108.3	1,095.7	107.7	1,203.4	43,076.1	2.8
1891	32.7	8.2	85.0	529.7	343.4	327.0	1,293.3	419.6	1,712.9	41,963.9	4.1
1892	33.4	15.0	53.4	691.4	501.0	66.8	1,327.6*	229.3	1,556.9	45,865.9	3.4
1893	33.2	18.3	39.8	836.6	448.2	132.8	1,475.7	494.1	1,969.8	49,408.5	4.0
1894	32.8	24.6	32.8	797.0	574.0	229.6	1,658.0*	263.7	1,921.7	52,738.3	3.6

[1] The years in which that part of the formula concerned with the loss by liquidations produced figures in excess of the known maximum loss by liquidation (see Table 20) are shown by an asterisk.

[2] The estimates of loss caused by writing down of capital are net of capital returned to shareholders as being "in excess of the wants of the company."

[3] The average annual loss to shareholders was 3.2 percent of the amount of capital at risk. An additional set of estimates (not reproduced here) based upon aggregated data produced a figure of 3.4 percent.

Sources: Col. (1) - Calculated from data contained in Tables 6 and 12.
Cols. (2) to (6) - Calculated from data contained in Table 4 in accordance with assumed percentage losses by liquidation as given in text.
Col. (8) - Estimates based upon data contained in the company files.
Col. (10) - Based upon Table 12

erroneous results (i.e. an annual figure for the "true loss" by liquidations greater than the known maximum loss incurred by company dissolutions,
see Table 20) be ignored on the grounds that the over estimates of loss
incurred in some years were probably balanced by under estimates in others,
these calculations indicate that the average annual rate of loss on the
paid-up capital of Scottish non-railway joint stock companies, 1870-1894,
was about 3.2 per cent, or approximately half of one per cent higher
than the 2.7 per cent that Macgregor estimated as being the rate of net
insolvency loss on the paid-up capital of British non-railway companies
for the period 1893-1902.[1]

An important question remains unanswered. What was the relationship
between the called-up capital of the early domestic Scottish joint stock
companies and the real investment undertaken by these companies?
Regrettably, the data contained in the company files are inadequate to
provide an answer. Only the most painstaking analysis of the internal
accounting records of each company could do this and such accounts have
rarely survived, far less been subjected to the necessary investigation.

However reluctant one may be to go beyond the capacity of the data
set, the circumstances invite conjecture. It has to be said, at the outset,
that because a relatively high proportion of the early Scottish limited
companies were conversions, the figures for paid-up capital within a year
of incorporation frequently imply little, if any, additional capital
formation. For example, when the firm of Merry & Cunninghame was formed

---

1. Macgregor, op.cit., pp.550-51; and see the illuminating discussion by
Michael Edelstein, "Realized Rates of Return on U.K. Home and Overseas
Portfolio Investment in the Age of High Imperialism", Explorations in
Economic History, XIII (1976), pp.296-98.

in 1872 with an issued capital of £1 million in shares and £500,000 in debentures, James Merry and the trustees of Alexander Cunninghame received £330,000 in fully paid-up ordinary shares, £300,000 5 per cent "B" debentures and £870,000 in cash. This procedure - which, of course, gave a considerable fillip to the figures of called-up capital in Scottish manufacturing companies - failed to contribute anything to gross capital formation. Merry & Cunninghame Ltd. emerged from the transaction with no more resources than had been possessed by the original partnership. The vendors received payment in shares, debentures and in cash (some of which may have found its way back into the manufacturing sector by subsequent re-investment); the investable funds of the limited company were not augmented. The conversion resulted in a legal change - the ownership of the firm had been altered - but, in itself, it had little or no immediate economic significance. Indeed, difficulties in meeting its cost obligation to James Merry brought about the voluntary liquidation of Merry & Cunninghame before the new directorate had apparently made any addition to the firm's capital assets. This case may be an extreme example but it does serve to illustrate the dangers of equating additional incrememts of called-up capital in joint stock enterprise with real investment, with capital formation. It is probable that many such changes in legal ownership in the second half of the nineteenth century did little to augment real investment expenditure for some time after the conversion had taken place.[1]

---

1. As Lavington observed of the decade or so before 1914, "the vast majority of the joint-stock companies coming into being each year are either already in possession of their capital or obtain it by way of private negotiation". F. Lavington, The English Capital Market (London: Methuen, 1921), p.202.

It was different with entirely new companies. Here, it is possible that a substantial part of the equity capital was transformed into productive assets. Evidence from the archives of the Steel Company of Scotland indicates that a very high proportion of the product of early calls was for the purpose of purchasing a site and erecting a steelworks at Hallside, near Glasgow. Within a year of incorporation, the contractual obligations of the company totalled approximately £97,000, or 92 per cent of the nominal, but as yet not fully called, capital of £105,000. Subsequent calls, together with substantial loans, were similarly transformed into dwelling houses for workmen and the erection of additional workshops, melting furnaces, rolling plant and steam hammers. By October 1877 total capital expenditure on the works exceeded £220,000 and the firm's nominal Ordinary capital had been increased almost fourfold to £500,000 with 34,480 £10 shares issued and £8 called on each share (£275,840), and of the £150,000 short-term debentures authorized, £100,000 had been issued to enable the directors to pay off advances by the Bank of Scotland.[1]

But this example may also be unrepresentative. Sir Charles Tennant and his associates, all well established and highly respected businessmen, experienced little difficulty in raising equity capital relatively inexpensively. Those who were lesser known; those proposing to exploit an original patent or intending to enter some new and relatively untried field of enterprise, might be expected to have incurred greater initial legal and promotional costs and to have employed a higher proportion of the product of their early calls on expenditures which did not involve

1. Payne, Colvilles ..., pp.23-32, 61.

any real investment; on, for example, the rental rather than the construction of factory or business premises or on the manufacture of prototypes utilizing machine tools and equipment purchased second-hand. Only if these initial activities were successful would it be possible for such a company to call up further funds for the purpose of capital formation.

So far attention has been directed to "manufacturing" companies (200-300). A similar spectrum of the consequences for capital formation doubtless attended the establishment of public utility companies. Many of the early single-ship companies (413) were motivated by a desire to minimise risk by owners of 64ths of ships already built.[1] In such cases, only a legal change was involved in the adoption of the limited company form; no purposeful capital investment followed incorporation. Latterly, of course, single-ship companies were formed expressly to build increasingly large and expensive iron and steel compound-engined vessels. Here, the called-up capital was almost entirely transformed into real capital and, despite substantial initial legal costs, the same was largely true of other classes of companies within the "public utility" division: the gas and water companies (432,433).

It is unnecessary to prolong this discussion. Its purpose has simply been to demonstrate that gross capital formation fell far short of the called-up capital of the early Scottish limited companies. There is too the problem of double counting. Many companies in the Finance, Insurance and Real Estate Division(800) employed part of their funds in the purchase

1. See above, p.67.

of ordinary shares of companies falling within other classes[1] and the assets of many holding companies comprised the equity of subsidiaries.

Taking a number of years at quinquennial intervals after 1875, an attempt was made to assess the magnitude of domestic capital formation that was a direct consequence of the initial issues of new Edinburgh-registered companies.[2] The results lend support to Giffen's observation, made in 1889, that "... the regular annual investment by individuals in their own business or properties, ... must always be the most important form of saving - far more important than the visible public investments".[3] Such was the significance of conversions (not so much in numbers as in size) and the flow of funds overseas, that it is possible that not more than 10 per cent to 20 per cent of the initial capital called up by new non-railway joint stock companies incorporated in Scotland was utilized in domestic fixed capital formation.[4] To be more precise would be spurious but, for what they are worth, the estimates produced figures of about

---

1. Although an examination of the records of a number of insurance companies established in Aberdeen indicates that Scottish insurance companies appear to have conformed to the national pattern of possessing extremely small holdings of ordinary stocks and shares. See D.K. Sheppard, The Growth and Role of U.K. Financial Institutions, 1880-1962 (London: Methuen, 1971), p.154.

2. It should be confessed that the use of the word "assess" is misleading: "guess" would be more accurate, though every attempt was made to make realistic assumptions in the estimating procedure. The basic statistical data were derived from materials summarized in Tables 4, 18, 19 and 20 and this was interpreted with information derived from the company files and from some twenty years' experience in analyzing Scottish business records. That is to say, the author has had to depend more heavily than he would wish on hunches.

3. R. Giffen, The Growth of Capital (London, 1889), pp.4, 153, quoted Michie, thesis, p.457.

4. In this connection, "initial" means the capital called up within a year or two of formal incorporation.

£200,000 in 1875, 1880 and 1885 and about £350,000 in 1890 and 1894.
Only in 1875 (24 per cent) did the proportion of called-up capital
invested in fixed capital assets appear to have exceeded 16 per cent;
in the other years the proportion varied between 9 per cent (1890) and
15.5 per cent (1880).

Having proceeded thus far, these conjectures may be pushed a little
further. Allowing that over the twenty-year period 1875-1894 Edinburgh-
registered companies represented 6 per cent of the total number of
companies incorporated in the United Kingdom (see Table 2), and assuming
that apart from a somewhat heavier bias towards overseas investment of
the London-registered companies, Scottish companies were tolerably
representative of those of the United Kingdom as a whole in both the
nature of their activities and in the proportion of their called-up
capital expended in the creation of new capital assets,[1] then the annual
gross domestic fixed capital formation attributable to new joint stock
companies in Great Britain may be estimated at some £3 million in the late
'seventies and 'eighties and at about £5 million in the early 'nineties.[2]
That is, gross domestic fixed capital formation by new United Kingdom joint

---

1. It is recognised that these are both heroic assumptions, see especially
   below, pp.108-9. It is, however, worth noting that Essex-Crosby found
   that in 1885 "the process of converting private family businesses into
   companies was only just beginning. £50,000,000 of capital had been
   converted in the decade 1875-84 and it was a movement which gathered
   impetus each year". A. Essex-Crosby, op.cit., p.24.

2. The estimation of these figures is based on the assumptions that
   (a) a little less than 60 per cent of the called-up capital of London-
   registered companies was for employment at home (see F. Lavington,
   op.cit., pp.206-7), compared with about 70 per cent in Scotland (see
   Table 19); (b) the proportion of called-up capital expended in the
   creation of new capital assets by Scottish companies was typical of
   all United Kingdom companies.

stock companies represented some 3 per cent of the nation's gross domestic fixed capital formation in the fifteen years up to the late 1880's and perhaps 5 per cent in the early 1890's.[1]

Estimates made by Lavington, Cairncross, Paish and Thomas[2] for the years immediately preceding the First World War indicate that these results are not implausible, but it is recognised that the figures presented here, like those of Lavington himself, are "open to considerable possibility of error".[3] With this reservation, they do point to the possibility that in the last quarter of the nineteenth century appreciably less than 10 per cent of real investment at home was financed through new issues on British stock exchanges by mining and manufacturing companies and public utilities, and that of this figure the proportion raised by new companies may have averaged between a half and two-thirds.[4] Relatively small though the proportion of real investment financed through new issues appears to be, it should perhaps be emphasized that the fact that companies could "go public" and, in effect, sell themselves to shareholders, must have made it easier to raise money for industrial and commercial purposes: the mere existence of a capital market must have contributed, albeit indirectly,

---

1. These proportions are derived from expressing my crude estimates of annual gross domestic fixed capital formation by joint-stock companies in the years 1875-1894 as a percentage of Feinstein's figures for gross domestic fixed capital formation at current prices for the United Kingdom for the same period. See C.H. Feinstein, National Income, Expenditure and Output of the United Kingdom, 1855-1965 (Cambridge: Cambridge University Press, 1972), Table 39, T85.

2. Lavington, op.cit., pp.204-6; A.K. Cairncross, Home and Foreign Investment, 1870-1913 (Cambridge: Cambridge University Press, 1953), pp.96-9; F.W. Paish, "The London New Issue Market", Economica, N.S. XVIII (1951), p.2; W.A. Thomas, The Provincial Stock Exchanges (London: Cass, 1973), p.139.

3. Lavington, op.cit., p.205.

4. This last conjecture is based on the calculations undertaken in connection with ascertaining the growth rates of Scottish companies (see above, Table 20 and pp.102-4); it receives some support from Jefferys' calculations, Business Organisation, pp.147-50; Appendix B. pp.452-3.

to the level of investment.[1]

V

SIZE, GROWTH, AND LENGTH OF LIFE

It has earlier been pointed out that the average length of life of
the Scottish companies formed between 1856 and 1895 and dissolved before
1975 was 16.4 years and that, however short a period this may at first
appear, it seems to have been longer than the average length of life of
London-registered companies.[2] In discussing company mortality, it has often
been assumed that in periods of economic crisis or depression it was the
younger and smaller companies that tended to be swept away. "As companies
grow older, their connections and goodwill expand and tend to keep them
stable and free from insolvency ... companies appear to reverse human
experience: with them, old age is partly a reason for expecting longer life".
This observation, by Shannon, carries with it the implication that there
exists some correlation between age and size: that older firms tend to be
bigger firms.[3] The later work of Hart and Prais indicated that during the
first fifty years of the twentieth century British firms expanded largely by
internal growth and that each increment of growth appeared to be associated
with a decrease in the probability of 'death'.[4] If this hypothesis is correct,
it has obvious implications for understanding the development of industrial
concentration, a subject which has recently been re-examined by Hannah and

---

1. I am indebted to Sir Alec Cairncross for drawing this point to my attention.

2. See above, pp.34-39.

3. Shannon, "The First Five Thousand ...", p.410. Shannon quotes Alfred
   Marshall, Principles of Economies, 8th ed. (London: Macmillan, 1920),
   p.316; "And as with the growth of trees, so was it with the growth of
   business as a general rule before the great recent development of vast
   joint stock companies which often stagnate but do not readily die."

4. P.E. Hart and S.J. Prais, "The Analysis of Business Concentration: A
   Statistical Approach", Journal of the Royal Statistical Society, Ser.
   A, 119 (1956), pp.168-75.

Kay.[1]

As the data collected during the course of this inquiry seemed to
have some relevance to these and related issues, an attempt was made to
answer the following questions: Was the life expectancy of the joint
stock companies incorporated in Scotland after 1856 a function of their
initial size, measured by their called-up capital? That is, did larger
firms live longer than smaller firms? And, second, was the rate of
growth of Scottish firms a function of their initial size? That is, did
firms which began active operations with a large capital grow proportionately
faster than those which started with a smaller capital?[2]

To pursue these related inquiries involved adopting an appropriate
definition of "initial size". Inspection of the data revealed that after
the first two or three years following the Act of 1856, few of the early
Scottish companies made any attempt to call up all the capital that they
evidently believed to be necessary for the successful inauguration of
their activities - or the extension of a firm previously organized as a
partnership - immediately upon incorporation. Rather, the great majority
made a systematic start: calling up the necessary proportion of their
authorized capital in stages. For example, a company incorporated with a

---

1. L. Hannah and J.A. Kay, Concentration in Modern Industry (London:
   Macmillan, 1977), especially Chapter 7, "The Gibrat Effect", pp.98-
   110. See also S.J. Prais, The Evolution of Giant Firms in Britain
   (Cambridge: Cambridge University Press, 1976) and P.E. Hart, "On
   Bias and Concentration", Journal of Industrial Economics, Vol.
   XXVII (1978-79), pp.211-26.

2. It was from the outset appreciated that called-up capital is not
   entirely satisfactory as a criterion of size, but it was the only
   criterion common to the company file data and most authorities
   recognize that issued, even nominal, capital does constitute a
   reasonable, if somewhat rough, indication of relative size. In
   the context of this paper, the fullest discussion of this question
   is that by G.H. Evans, op.cit., pp.42, 172-4.

nominal capital of £10,000 in, say October 1870, typically would have
called up about £2,000 during the remaining months of 1870 (of which
perhaps half would represent the amount considered as paid up on
vendors' shares), £1,000 during 1871, and not until the Autumn of 1872,
when the called-up capital figure stood at about £3,500, would periodic
calls on the shareholders cease. Only if the business proved successful
would calls resume; perhaps, in this hypothetical example, in 1876.
It was therefore decided that the initial size of each company might
best be measured by the amount of capital called up within three years
of the date of incorporation, although the volume of capital called up
before the last day of the year in which incorporation took place was
not ignored.[1]

It was now possible to proceed to a series of least squares
regressions[2] of the form

$$Y = \beta'x$$

where, in answering the first question, the dependent variable, Y, was
length of life and x, the independent variable, was either the capital
called up within the year of incorporation, k_1, or k_1 and the capital
called up within three years of incorporation, k_3. The results may
be summarized as follows:

---

1. Very little was expected of calculations based upon this latter
   figure since a company incorporated in, say, February, would have
   had a much greater opportunity to raise its required capital than
   a company incorporated late in November or in December.

2. I must, once again, express my indebtedness to Professor Forrest
   D. Nelson for invaluable assistance in carrying out these computa-
   tions.

TABLE 22

REGRESSIONS OF THE LENGTH OF LIFE OF SCOTTISH COMPANIES ON THE SIZE OF
COMPANIES

(a) <u>Life on k_1</u>

	R^2	0.0088
	Standard Error	229.5
	Overall F $(1,2411)$	21.3

Variable	B	Standard Error	F
k_1	0.000304	0.00007	21.2752
Constant	206.307		

(b) <u>Life on k_1 & k_3</u>

	R^2	0.0118
	Standard Error	229.2
	Overall F $(2,2410)$	14.4

Variable	B	Standard Error	F
k_3	0.000367	0.00013	7.475
k_1	-0.000077	0.00015	0.249
Constant	205.0317		

These data indicate that the mere size of a company at birth or within
three years of birth had a negligible influence on its expectation of life
in its original form,[1] at most 1.2 per cent of the variance in life is
explained by initial size. Other factors were vastly more important: the

---

1. It is worth emphasizing that when a firm went into voluntary liquidation
   for reconstruction, sale or amalgamation, it officially "died" (i.e. it
   was dissolved), even though it may have enjoyed a continuing existence
   under another name or in a different organizational or structural form.

nature of the firm's activities, the quality of its direction and management, the state of the economic invironment within which it operated, and so on.[1] To illustrate the influence of the first of these, Table 23 shows the average length of life of companies in various industrial categories. Not surprisingly, public utilities involved in the supply of gas, water and electricity had by far the longest lives.[2] Real estate companies and textile firms also enjoyed life spans substantially longer than the average. The speculative nature of overseas ventures in mining and quarrying is revealed, while the relatively short lives of chemical firms is explicable in terms of contemporary merger activity. The possibility that the economic climate prevailing during the year of incorporation might have been influential in determining infant and adult health was tested, but the hypothesis that more robust firms might have been brought into being during periods of depression - when both promoters and shareholders were more likely to have been more careful in establishing and supporting concerns - received little support from the generalized data presented in Table 7. The fact is that to explain company longevity necessitates going beyond numerical aggregates to the quality of entrepreneurship possessed by company directorates, and data on this intangible factor is not to be found in the company files.

---

1. In commenting on an earlier draft, Dr. W.P. Kennedy made the point that although these results undoubtedly show that factors other than size at birth were collectively more important in the determination of the length of life of a firm, so many other factors were relevant that size at birth may have been as important as any other single factor.

2. Henry Lowenfeld observed in 1909 that "Railways, Banks, Insurance Companies, Breweries, Telephone, Waterworks, Gas, Telegraph, and Shipping Companies as a rule live long, whilst Mineral Water, Drapery, Cycle, Mining and Oil Companies generally have short lives". H. Lowenfeld, All About Investment (London, 1909), p.185.

TABLE 23

AVERAGE LENGTH OF LIFE OF DISSOLVED SCOTTISH COMPANIES
BY SELECTED INDUSTRIAL CLASSIFICATIONS

Industrial Classification	Brief Description	Average Length of Life in Years
120	Coal Mining	20.9
116,151,152	Overseas Companies in Mining & Quarrying	6.4
210-230	Manufacturing: Food, Drink & Tobacco	17.2
240,250,262	Manufacturing: Textiles, Clothing & Footwear	21.1
300	Manufacturing: Paper & Allied Products	16.6
320	Manufacturing: Chemicals & Allied Products	10.0
340	Manufacturing: Iron & Steel & Products	14.8
360	Manufacturing: Machinery	12.7
370	Manufacturing: Transportation Equipment	11.9
410	Public Utilities: Transportation	13.4
430	Public Utilities: Electricity, Gas & Water	36.1
610-690	Retail Trade	13.6
810-870	Finance & Insurance	17.7
880	Real Estate	24.9
900	Agricultural, Forestry & Fishing	13.6
100-900	ALL DISSOLVED COMPANIES	16.4

In attempting to answer the second question: whether the rate of growth of Scottish firms was a function of initial size, the statistical data also produced negative results. After companies with lives longer than three calendar years were selected, the growth rate (Y) was computed so that

$$Y = \frac{k_f - k_3}{\text{Life}.k_3}$$

where

k_f = final capital, i.e. the called-up capital during the last month of a company's existence in its original form;

k_3 = the capital called up after three calendar years;

and Life = the length of a company's life in months.

The growth rate, Y, was then regressed on k_3 for all those companies surviving for over three years in each of the following major industrial groups: (a) Mining and Quarrying (Industrial Classification: 100-152), (b) Manufacturing (I.C.: 200-390), (c) Public Utilities (I.C.: 400-446), (d) Wholesale and Retail Trade (I.C.: 500-690), (e) Service Trades (I.C.: 700-740), (f) Finance, Insurance and Real Estate (I.C.: 800-890), and (g) Agriculture, Forestry and Fishing (I.C.: 900-920). Once again, the results may be summarized in tabular form (Table 24).

As in the previous examination of the influence of birth size on life expectancy, these data show that whatever else it was that determined the growth rate of Scottish incorporated firms in the second half of the nineteenth century, it was not the initial called-up capital, which at most (in Mining and Quarrying) explained about 3 per cent of the subsequent growth of companies within the major industrial groups. Somewhat

TABLE 24

REGRESSIONS OF GROWTH RATES OF SCOTTISH COMPANIES SURVIVING MORE THAN THREE YEARS ON THE SIZE OF COMPANIES, BY MAJOR INDUSTRIAL GROUPS

(a) Growth Rate of Mining and Quarrying Companies on k_3

R^2 0.0024
Standard Error 0.0123
Overall F (1,272) 0.643

Variable	B	Standard Error	F
k_3	-0.000069	0.00009	0.643
Constant	0.00238		

(b) Growth Rate of Manufacturing Companies on k_3

R^2 0.0011
Standard Error 0.0219
Overall F (1,704) 0.755

Variable	B	Standard Error	F
k_3	-0.000085	0.00010	0.755
Constant	0.00279		

(c) Growth Rate of Public Utility Companies on k_3

R^2 0.00097
Standard Error 0.00967
Overall F (1,659) 0.637

Variable	B	Standard Error	F
k_3	-0.000059	0.00007	0.637
Constant	0.00129		

(d) Growth Rate of Wholesale and Retail Trading Companies on k_3

R^2 0.0025
Standard Error 0.0047
Overall F (1,97) 0.243

Variable	B	Standard Error	F
k_3	-0.000056	0.00011	0.243
Constant	0.00135		

(e) Growth Rate of Service Companies on k_3

R^2 0.00004
Standard Error 0.0036
Overall F (1,254) 0.00902

Variable	B	Standard Error	F
k_3	-0.00026	0.00027	0.009
Constant	0.00105		

(f) Growth Rate of Finance, Insurance & Real Estate Companies on k_3

R^2 0.00064
Standard Error 0.0828
Overall F (1,282) 0.1800

Variable	B	Standard Error	F
k_3	-0.00016	0.00037	0.180
Constant	0.0092		

(g) Growth Rate of Agricultural, Forestry & Fishing Companies on k_3

R^2 0.0000
Standard Error 0.0037
Overall F (1,120) 0.00023

Variable	B	Standard Error	F
k_3	0.0000007	0.00005	0.0002
Constant	0.00112		

surprisingly, it must be concluded that the incidence of factors which
brought about growth and decline in firms which retained their original
form (i.e. those which were not dissolved as a preparatory step to
participating in a merger) was unrelated to the initial size of the firm[1]
and that therefore these data are not inconsistent with - perhaps even
support - the apparently implausible assumptions of Gibrat's law of
proportionate effect.[2]

VI

GAINS AND LOSSES

In past studies of the British limited joint stock companies, much
has been made of the failures: "The companies wound up compulsorily or
under supervision or by reason of liabilities ... within five years of
registration. /For these companies7 it is reasonable to assume that ...
investors lost all, or almost all, the capital sunk."[3] Or again, "If a

---

1. It is not known whether a different result would have been produced had
it been possible to overcome the informational inadequacies and technical
difficulties involved in assuming continuity between firms of the same
or of a similar name but of a changing legal form and composition. (It
would involve the assumption, for example, that the Clyde Tube Works,
A. & J. Stewart, A. & J. Stewart Ltd., incorporated as a private company
in 1882, A. & J. Stewart and Clydesdale Ltd., 1890, A. & J. Stewart &
Menzies Ltd., 1898, and Stewarts & Lloyds, 1903, were essentially one
and the same firm /for the antecedents of Stewarts & Lloyds, see Payne,
Colvilles ..., pp.92-67). One can hardly avoid the presumption that it
would, but one cannot be sure.

2. For the assumptions underlying Gibrat's law, see Hannah and Kay, op.
cit., pp.98-101. Perhaps the clearest statement of the law is that by
P.E. Hart: "The determinants of the growth of firms tend to change the
size of firms by randomly distributed proportions. Some forces make for
an increase, some for a decrease, but all act randomly in the sense that
there is no tendency to favour or disfavour firms of any particular
size." P.E. Hart, Studies in Profit, Business Saving and Investment in
the United Kingdom, 1920-1962 (London: Allen & Unwin, 1965), pp.150-51.
Hart's entire discussion of "Growth and the Size of Firm" (pp.150-180)
should be consulted.

3. Shannon, "The Limited Companies", p.295, and see p.302.

balance sheet could be drawn up of the losses and gains to Great Britain
from the establishment of companies on the limited principle to work
industrial undertakings, we have no doubt the balance would be largely on
the wrong side."[1] But, as Edelstein has so justly remarked, "A study of
returns to financial capital should optimally involve analysis of both
failures and successes."[2] Ideally, estimates of capital loss should be set
against the returns yielded by investment in the great mass of companies,
insufficient and incompetent though many of them may have been, that
attempted to attain the objectives outlined in their Memoranda of
Association. The company files rarely provide such information nor, with
certain exceptions, can it be obtained elsewhere.[3] Few records have
survived of the majority of those companies which were in fact, if not in
law, private companies. The only relevant data fairly readily available are
the dividends paid on publicly traded shares and there is no satisfactory
manner of judging whether or not they were representative; I suspect that
over time they were on the low side.[4]

---

1. Economist, 37(1879), p.1254, quoted by Shannon, "The Limited Companies",
    p.295n.

2. M. Edelstein, "Realized Rates of Return on U.K. Home and Overseas
    Portfolio Investment", p.286.

3. Ibid., p.287. Because of data limitations, Edelstein was forced to
    restrict his attention to a relatively narrow range of publicly traded,
    first- and second-class equity, preference, and debenture instruments.
    Some of the implications of this are discussed by W.P. Kennedy,
    "Institutional Response to Economic Growth", loc.cit., pp.174-6.

4. Where inspection of the ledgers of nineteenth century Scottish private
    companies has been possible, the annual dividends that they reveal
    were, at times, surprisingly high, frequently exceeding 15 per cent.

At present, it is impossible to say precisely how far the net losses incurred in liquidations were compensated for by the returns received by investors before dissolution took place. But if the general validity of Edelstein's judicious estimate of 6-9 per cent per annum as the average return on British manufacturing and commercial equity be accepted (and this figure would, it is argued, have been exceeded by the average return on overseas investment),[1] it would appear that on the whole the possessor of a diversified portfolio of shares in the Scottish companies incorporated during the second half of the nineteenth century benefitted financially from his investment. He might well have received a <u>net</u> return of about 3-4 per cent,[2] the real value of which would undoubtedly have been boosted by prevailing price trends.[3] Not startling perhaps, but enough to inspire the belief that the financial gains almost certainly outweighed the losses.

In drawing up any balance sheet of "the gains and losses from the establishment of companies on the limited principle", it is not enough to

1. Edelstein, "Realized Rates of Return", p.291. The general magnitude of these figures is broadly confirmed by the fragmentary data contained in the files of the dissolved Scottish companies.

2. This figure is based upon a number of admittedly rough calculations which took into account (i) the general direction of Scottish joint stock activity (i.e. its distribution between major industrial groups and between domestic and overseas ventures), (ii) the average length of life of Edinburgh-registered companies, (iii) the estimated capital losses incurred through liquidations - all of which have been previously discussed - and, (iv) the spotty dividend and balance sheet data derived from the company files and from other primary and secondary sources. The biases embodied in these somewhat crude attempts to assess the general magnitude of the net return to shareholders have been downwards.

3. The Rousseaux Price Indices, reproduced in B.R. Mitchell, <u>Abstract of British Historical Statistics</u> (Cambridge: Cambridge University Press, 1962), pp.472-3, reveal a markedly falling price trend during the period covered by this paper, especially from the early 'seventies onwards. This would have increased the real value of the return on investment which would have been only partially offset by increases in the real value of capital losses.

consider only the direct financial return on equities. It is a
peculiarity of many forms of investment that the benefits accruing to
the community often exceed those to the shareholder. The limited company,
whatever its initial weaknesses, however much it disappointed the hopes
of its proponents in the mid-'fifties, played a significant role in
permitting the continued evolution and diversification of the Scottish
economy in the later half of the nineteenth century and in generally
improving the standard of life of the Scottish people. It is unnecessary
to elaborate this point. It is enough to draw attention to such themes
as the greater stability of Scottish banking following the adoption of
limited liability after the failure of the City of Glasgow Bank; the
remarkable progress made in the heavy industries, in steel-making, shipbuilding and marine engineering; the cutting of freignt charges brought
about by competition between shipping companies; the massive reduction
in the prices of many of the staple foodstuffs following upon the rapid
development of the pastoral areas of North America and Australia; the
greatly enhanced provision of public amenities, gas, water, electricity,
public halls and cemeteries. All these and many more factors in
improving the quality of life of the multitude stemmed to a greater or
lesser extent from the adoption of the limited joint stock company form
of business organization. They surely deserve some place in any balance
sheet of gains and losses?

CONCLUSION

This essay has tried to do for the early Scottish limited companies what Shannon and others have already done for the London-registered companies. Only inasmuch as an attempt had been made to achieve a greater precision and a deeper level of analysis than earlier writers on this general theme - the general setting for which continues to be Jefferys' enduring study of <u>Business Organization in Great Britain, 1856-1914</u> - is there any real difference. A question which remains to be asked is whether the Scottish experience was simply a regional reflection of the British whole. Any attempt to provide a definite solution is inhibited by a lack of comparable data, but a provisional answer would be "not entirely so". In this, as in so many other facets of economic and social history, Scotland was somewhat different. The Scottish limited companies appear to have been smaller, to have enjoyed a more lengthy existence, to have been less bedevilled by fraud, ignorance and gross mismanagement, and to have been controlled by their founders a little longer than their English counterparts; and they probably produced a marginally higher net return to their shareholders. Yet in other respects one cannot help believing that a like analysis of the London-registered companies would produce similar results. For example, the influence of the trade cycle on the timing of promotional and incorporation activity appears to have been much the same in Scotland, England and America, and there seems to be no reason to expect that the relationship between initial capital size, life and the rate of growth would have been different had the analysis been of

English companies.[1] Furthermore, were it possible to analyse a complete collection of English companies traded on an important provincial exchange the similarities with Scotland might well be remarkable.[2]

Whatever proves to be the case, this essay will have achieved its purpose if its underlying data has some value for economic historians and if its methods possess some utility for future inquiries by either historians or economists into what might be called institutional demography.

---

1. Belief in the validity of this point has been encouraged by an observation by Macgregor, op.cit., pp.503-4, that "Taking only the nominal capitalizations of all companies registered in 1890, the five-year survival is only two points per cent worst for all companies capitalized at over £20,000 than for all companies capitalized at over £100.000."

2. See the point made above,p.49n.

CATEGORIES USED IN CLASSIFYING COMPANIES

100 Mining and Quarrying

  110 Metal Mining

    111 Iron

    112 Copper and Sulphur

    113 Lead and Zinc

    114 Gold and Silver

    115 Other metals

    116 *Overseas companies engaged in the above categories*

    117 Unallocable

  120 Coal Mining

  140 Nonmetallic mining and quarrying

    141 Stone, sand and gravel (including granite, slate, marble and limestone)

    142 Other mining and quarrying (including clay, asbestos, mica, rock salt, peat cutting and processing)

  150 Those engaged in combinations of the above activities and/or including the working of nitrate deposits

    151 *Overseas companies in this category (Colonial)*

    152 *Overseas companies in this category (Foreign)*

200/300 Manufacturing

  210 Food and kindred products

    211 Bakery products

    212 Confectionary and related products (including chocolate and cocoa products)

    213 Canning and preserving fruits, vegetables and seafoods

    214 Meat products

    215 Grain-mill products

    216 Dairy products

    217 Sugar

    218 Others (including combinations of the above activities)

    219 *Overseas ventures in the above categories*

  220 Beverages

    221 Malt and malt liquors

    222 Distilled, rectified and blended liquors

    223 Wines

    224 Nonalcoholic beverages

    225 Others (including those not allocable)

  230 Tobacco manufacturers (including snuff)

  240 Textile-mill products

    241 Cotton

    242 Woolen and worsted

    243 Silk

    244 Linen, flax, hemp and jute

    245 Rope works and sail manufacture

    246 Knitted goods (including hosiery)

    247 Carpets

    248 Dyeing and finishing textiles

    249 *Overseas ventures in the above categories*

  250 Apparel and other finished products made from fabrics

    251 Men's and boys' clothing

    252 Women's, children's and infants' clothing

    253 Fur goods

    254 Millinery

    255 Other apparel

    256 Unallocable

  260 Leather and leather products

    261 Leather: tanned, cured and finished

    262 Footwear (except rubber)

    263 Other leather products

  270 Rubber, gutta-percha and vulcanite products

  280 Lumber and timber basic products (see also categories 916-17; i.e., those produced in sawmills)

290 Furniture and finished timber products
  291 Furniture
  292 Wooden containers (including barrels, casks and boxes, often bound in metal)
  293 Others (including matches and cork products)

300 Paper and Allied Products (including mill board)

310 Printing, publishing and allied industries
  311 Book publishers
  312 Newspapers, periodicals and journals
  313 Unallocable

320 Chemicals and allied products
  321 Paints, varnishes, polishes, timber preservatives and colours
  322 Soap and glycerine
  323 Drugs, toilet preparations and insecticides
  324 Fertilizers
  325 Animal and vegetable oils (tallow, lard and stearine)
  326 Shale oil: distillation and refining of crude oil into refined products (e.g., paraffin) from shale, coal, etc.
  327 Others (including industrial chemicals and metal extraction from ores)
  328 Explosives and gunpowder
  329 Overseas ventures in the above categories (including oil wells and petroleum refining)

330 Stone, clay and glass products
  331 Brick, tile and other structural clay products
  332 Pottery and related products
  333 Glass and glass products
  334 Cement
  335 Concrete, gypsum and plaster products
  336 Others (including abrasives, asbestos products and cut stone)
  337 Unallocable
  338 Overseas ventures in the above categories

340 Iron and steel and their products
  341 Blast furnaces, steel works and rolling mills
  342 Fabricated structural steel and ornamental metal work
  343 Light rolled products and tinplate
  344 Tools and general ironmongery (except machine tools and cutlery)
  345 Heating apparatus (except electric), enameled-iron sanitary ware and boiler-shop products
  346 Others (including cast iron pipes, cutlery, foundry and wires products) [See also 362]
  348 Overseas ventures in the above categories

350 Nonferrous metals and their products and electrical machinery
  352 Jewellery
  353 Others
  354 Electrical machinery and apparatus (including light bulbs)

360 Machinery (except electrical)
  361 Special industrial machinery (usually made under patents)
  362 General industrial machinery (including those produced by companies possessing both a foundry and machine shop)
  363 Metal working and wood working machinery
  364 Engines and turbines
  365 Construction and mining machinery
  366 Agricultural machinery, steam tractors and ploughs
  367 Office and shop machines, equipment and supplies
  368 Others (including refrigerators, sewing machines, gas purification plant, water and gas meters)

370 Transportation equipment
  371 Railway equipment (including locomotives)
  372 Railway rolling stock
  373 Ship and boat building
  374 Specialized parts of vessels (e.g., stern frames, propellers and anchors)
  375 Dry docks and slipways
  376 Bicycles and parts
  377 Others (including carts and wheelbarrows)
  378 Unallocable (including those involved in combinations of the above activities)

APPENDIX TABLE 1 (continued)

380 Miscellaneous manufacturing industries

381 Ice

382 Others (including professional and scientific instruments, photographic apparatus, toys, guns and ammunitions, and articles combining metal, glass and wooden components)

383 Linoleum and floor cloth combining textiles, cork, oil, etc.

400 Public Utilities

410 Transportation

411 Ocean shipping

412 Coastal shipping, tug and pilot boat companies and salvage companies

413 Single ship companies

414 Railways

415 Railways (Colonial)

416 Railways (Foreign)

417 Tram companies and road steam engines for urban haulage

418 Omnibus companies for passengers and parcels, freight carriers and job masters

419 Canal operation and ferries

420 Communication: telephones and telegraph and overseas ventures

421 Overseas ventures in coastal and river shipping, omnibus companies and the like

422 Overseas ventures in telegraphy (Colonial)

423 Overseas ventures in telegraphy (Foreign)

430 Other public utilities

431 Electric light and power

432 Gas production and distribution and by-products (including coke)

433 Water

435 Piers, harbors and shipways

436 Others (including weigh bridges, sewage and tunnels)

439 Overseas ventures in the above categories (Foreign)

440 Public halls, house construction and renovation, and cemeteries

441 Assembly halls and drill halls

442 Produce exchanges, collections of shops and bazaars

443 Building and improvement of the dwellings of the working class

444 Cooperative building companies (i.e., petty masons, joiners and plumbers joining together)

445 Builders and contractors

446 Cemeteries

500 Wholesale Trade

510 Merchant wholesalers

511 Companies established specifically for overseas trade

512 Companies established specifically for trading in agricultural produce or in the products required by farmers, including auctioneers specializing in such products

520 Commission merchants, manufacturers' agents, merchandise brokers, wharfingers and general warehousemen

530 Others (including those who combine the functions under categories 510 and 520)

600 Retail

610 Department, general merchandise and grocery stores

611 Cooperative ventures, especially stores

620 Food

630 Chemists and druggists

690 Others (including hardware, house furnishings and furniture, coal yards, book shops and tobacconists)

700 Service

710 Domestic and personal

711 Hotels, boarding houses, cafés, coffee houses, restaurants and temperance establishments

712 Laundries

713 Photographic studios

714 Others (including public bath houses and undertaking establishments)

720 Business services (e.g., advertising, packing, stevedores, trade protection societies, etc.)

722 Overseas ventures (Foreign)

APPENDIX TABLE 1 (continued)

730 Amusement and entertainment (including theatres, opera houses, sports and social clubs)

740 Others (including political, charitable and religious organizations, schools, colleges, hospitals, hydropathic establishments, companies to operate museums and exhibitions, mechanics' institutes, reading rooms, swimming baths and public parks)

800 Finance, Insurance and Real Estate

810 Commercial banks and trust companies

820 Building societies

830 Mortgage, heritable property and feuing companies
   831 Home
   832 Colonial
   833 Foreign

840 Investment trusts and companies
   841 Home
   842 Colonial
   843 Foreign

850 Stock brokers and investment bankers

860 Finance companies and industrial and personal loan companies
   861 Petty money-lending

870 Insurance, life assurance and annuity companies
   871 Insurance against diseases of, and accidents to, cattle

880 Real estate (including urban improvements)
   881 Home
   882 Foreign
   883 Colonial

890 Those not allocable to the above categories (including general auctioneers, patent holding companies)
   891 Colonial
   892 Foreign

900 Agricultural, Forestry and Fishing

910 Agriculture (including threshing and cultivation and haulage by steam power and other such agricultural aids)
   911 Home
   912 Colonial
   913 Foreign
   914 Ranching (i.e., land and cattle companies): Colonial
   915 Ranching: Foreign
   916 Forestry and lumbering (i.e., land and timber companies): Colonial
   917 Forestry and lumbering: Foreign

920 Fishing
   921 Fishing and dealing in fish, curing, processing waste parts of fish, distribution, etc.
   922 Fishing: British inshore waters
   923 Fishing: deep sea, including sealing and whaling

APPENDIX TABLE 2

AN INDUSTRIAL CLASSIFICATION OF SCOTTISH JOINT STOCK COMPANIES FORMED
BETWEEN 1856 AND JUNE 1895

NOTES:

1. For major category totals, see Table 14
2. Figures given some of the sub-groups (i.e., those with a classification number which is a multiple of ten but not of one hundred) include the number of companies which could not properly be more precisely defined. For example, where the figures for companies formed in the category 510 do not equal the sum of 511 and 512, the difference is made up of companies which could not be described more accurately than "merchant wholesalers" (category 510).

Mining & Quarrying — 100; Metal (110 = 111–117); 120; Nonmetal (140 = 141, 142); 150, 151*, 152*. Manufacturing — Food & Kindred Products (200–300; 210 = 211–219*).

Year	100	110	111	112	113	114	115	116*	117	120	140	141	142	150	151*	152*	200–300	210	211	212	213	214	215	216	217	218	219*
1856	1									1							3	1	1								
1857	1										1	1					7	2	1				1				
1858	1	1	1														2	1	1								
1859																											
1860	3	1		1						1	1	1					3	1						1			
1861	5	3		2		1								2			5	1	1								
1862	6	6		3	3												3	1	1								
1863	3	2							2					1			4	1	1								
1864	1													1			4										
1865	1	1							1								12										
1866	3	1			1						2	2					16										
1867																	2										
1868	5	1							1		1	1		3		1	2										
1869											1	1			1												
1870	2	1			1									1			3	1						1			
1871	4	2						1	1					2			13	1	1								
1872	18	4						4		8	2	2		4		3	26										
1873	17	4						4		3	6	3	3	4	1	3	16	1						1			
1874	8	2				1		1		3	2	2		1		1	11	1	1						1		1
1875	6	2						2		2	1	1		1			9										
1876	9	4		1				3		2	2	2		1			15										
1877	5	1			1						3	2	1	1			15	2					1	1			
1878	4	2						2		1				1			13	1					1				1
1879	6	2		1				1		3				1			9										
1880	2									2						1	20	2	1				1				
1881	7	1							1	3	1		1	2			22	5			1		1				
1882	8	3						2	1	3	2	2			1		24	1		1						1	
1883	8	5						5		1	1	1		1			35	3	1				1	1			
1884	10	6			1			5		2	2	2				1	43	5	1		1			1			
1885	6	1						1		3	2	2					24										
1886	8	3						3		2	2	2		1			31	2	1				1	1			
1887	7	2						2		4	1	1					30	2	1				1				
1888	9	7		1				6		2							41	6			1		1	1	1	1	
1889	20	11						11		7	1	1		1			47	6		1			1	1			1
1890	17	8				1		7		5	3	2	1	1		1	59	4			1		1	1			
1891	7	3						3		3	1		1				65	9			1		2	1		3	
1892	13	6						6		1	1	1		5	2	3	64	2		1			1	1			2
1893	20	2						2		10	4	2	2	4	2		70	3		1	1			1		1	
1894	27	15				1	2	12		10				2	2	1	65	8	1	3	1	1	1		1		1
1895	18	10						9	1	6	2	1	1		1	1	49	5						2	1	1	
Total	297	123	1	9	7	4	2	92	8	88	45	35	10	41	10	16	882	78	14	7	7	1	16	15	4	8	6

* Indicates overseas ventures.

APPENDIX TABLE 2 (continued)

(continued)

Year	Manufacturing 220	Beverages 221	222	223	224	225	230	240	241	242	243	Textiles 244	245	246	247	248	249*	250	Clothing 251	252	253	254	255	256	260	Leather 261	262	263	270
1856																													
1857																													1
1858																													
1859																													
1860																													
1861																													1
1862								1				1																	
1863																													
1864																													
1865	1	1						3	1	2																			
1866	1	1						2	1	1		1					1												
1867								1										1						1					
1868																													
1869																													
1870																													
1871	1							1				1													1	1			
1872		1						2									1								1	1			
1873								3				1	1				1								1	1			
1874	1				1			1									1												
1875								3	1	1						1													
1876	2	1	2					3	2			1																	
1877	2		1																										
1878																2													1
1879								2	1																				
1880			1					1	1				1					1	1										
1881							1	3	1			1																	
1882	2		1		1			1		1						1											1		1
1883	3		1		2			10	2			4	1			1	1								1		1		1
1884	1							3	1			1	1			1	1								1				1
1885			1		2																								
1886	4	1	2			1	1	3	1			1	1			1													
1887	3	1	2					3				1						1						1					1
1888	4	1	2		2			6	1	1			1	1		3	2								1		1		
1889	8	2	1		1			4		1		2																	1
1890	4	2	4			1		6	2	1		2				1		1								1			1
1891	3	1	2					5					1			2		1											
1892	5	2			2	1		10										1		1					1				
1893	10	1	8		1			9		2		6				2		1						1	1		1		1
1894	14	3	10			1	1	8	1	1		3			1	1													1
1895	10	5	5		1			4	1	1		3			1	1													1
Total	83	23	43	0	13	4	3	98	18	13	0	29	7	1	2	17	8	7	1	1	0	0	0	3	9	4	4	0	11

Manufacturing

Year	280	290 Wood Products			300	310 Publishing			320	Chemicals & Allied Products									330	Stone, Clay & Glass						
		291	292	293		311	312	313		321	322	323	324	325	326	327	328	329*		331	332	333	334	335	336	337	338
1856						1	1		1	1																	
1857						1	1												1		1						
1858																											
1859																											
1860						1			2				1				1		1								
1861						1	1		1						1	1											
1862					1		1		1						1	1											
1863									2							1											
1864									2							1		1	1								
1865					1				10						9	1			2								
1866					1																						
1867					1																						
1868																											
1869						1	1		2					1	3	1	1	1	1	1					1	1	
1870		1				1	1	1	6	1	1		1		2	1	1	1	2	1					1	1	
1872	1		1			2	1		5	1	1		1		2	1											
1873	1	1			3	1	1	1														1					
1874			1			1	1		1							1			1						1		
1875					1		1																				
1876						4	4	1	3						1		1										
1877					1	4	3		3		1				1	2	1		1		1					1	
1878	1				1	1	1		4						2												
1879															1				1								
1880					2	3	2	1	6						2	4			3			1					
1881						2	2		1	1	1		1		1		1	1	5	3	2	1					1
1882	1							1	4		1				5												
1884		2	2		1	2	1	1	6	1		1	1		2	3		2	2	2							
1885		2	1		2	3	2		8	3					2	4	1	1	2								
1886						3	3		11	1	1	1				2											
1887		1			2	2	1		7	1			2		1	2			2	1					1		
1888					1	3	1	1	4		1				4	4			3			2				1	
1889			1		2	6	1	1	4	1		1		1		2	1		2	2							
1890	2				2	5	2	1	6	2		2			1	3			2		1						
1891		2	1			7		3	7			2	1	1		4	1	1	3			1	1				1
1892		4	3		3	6		3	9	2	1	3				4			1			1	1	1			
1893	6	2	1		2	7		7	13	1	1	1	1	1	3	2			5	4		1					
1894	1	3	2			1	1	1	7		1	1				2			2	2		1	1		1		
1895		1		1	5	5	1	2	5			1				4		1	5	3		1					
Total	13	5	14	1	28	76	10	49	15	146	14	6	12	7	4	38	47	7	6	40	16	4	8	2	1	4	3	2

APPENDIX TABLE 2 (continued)

(continued)

Year	Manufacturing 340	Iron & Steel 341	342	343	344	345	346	347	348*	350 Nonferrous	352	353	354	360	361	362	Machinery (except Electrical) 363	364	365	366	367	368	369
1856	1																						
1857							1																
1858																						1	
1859														1									
1860																	1						
1861														1									
1862																							
1863																						1	
1864																							
1865	1																			1		1	
1866				1										2									
1867																							
1868																							
1869														1	1								
1870																							
1871																							
1872	6	5						1						3	2	1							
1873	2	2												1	1								
1874					2									2	2	2							
1875														2	2								
1876														2	2	1				1			
1877	1		1											2	1	1							
1878					1		1							2	1	1		1					
1879	1	1										1		1	1			1					
1880	1	1								1				1	1								
1881	4	2								1			1	2									
1882		1			1	1	1			3		1		3	2	1							1
1883	1	1					1						2	4	4								
1884	4	1	1		1	1	1	1		4	1		3	6	3	2		1					
1885	1	1	1											2	2	1							
1886	4	2				1		1	1	2			2	3	1	2		1					
1887	3	1				1		1						5	1	2					1		
1888	3	1	1							2			3	2	2	2					1	1	1
1889	3	1								4		1		8	2			1		1		1	
1890	5	2				2	1			1			1	6	1	8							
1891										1		1		15	6	6							
1892	8	1	1		2		3							8	1	6					1		
1893	2	1	1							2			2	6	2	4					1		
1894	4	1	1		1	2	1							12	6	4		1	1	1	1		1
1895	3	2			1			1				1		6	1							1	1
Total	63	24	7	1	6	8	10	6	1	19	1	4	14	107	41	40	2	6	1	3	5	5	4

Column groups — Manufacturing: **370 Transportation Equipment** (370–378), **380 Miscellaneous** (380–383). Public Utilities: **400**, **410 Transportation** (410–419), **420 Communication** (420–423).

Year	370	371	372	373	374	375	376	377	378	380	381	382	383	400	410	411	412	413	414	415*	416*	417	418	419	420	421*	422*	423
1856	1	1												5	4	3	1											
1857														8	2	1							1					
1858														10	1		1											
1859														5	1	1												
1860														7	2		2											
1861	2		1	1										11	2	1	1						1					
1862														14											1	1		
1863														10	3	1	1						1		1			
1864	1			1										14	8	2	6								2			
1865	2			1		1								13	4		3								2			1
1866	1								1	1		1		12	3		2						1					
1867														10	3		3											
1868														9	2	1	1											
1869														9	2	2												
1870														6	1	1												
1871	2		2							2	1	1		17	3	1	1						2					
1872	3			1	1				1	1	1			20	10	4	3						1		1			
1873														12	2	1	1					1	1					
1874	1			1										16	3	1	1		1				1					
1875	2	1		1										11	2	1	1					1	1		1	1		
1876	1			1										15	1	1	2					1						
1877	1			1										17	5	2	2											
1878										1		1		10	1	1	1											
1879	1			1						1		1		15	7	2	4					1			2			
1880	1				1					2		2		12	4	2	2			1					2		1	
1881														21	12	2	3	7										
1882	1	1								2		2		36	26	6	3	15					1	1				
1883	3	1	1	1						2		2		32	25	5	2	18				1						
1884	2	1		1						1		1		23	14	3	1	8		1			2					
1885	1			1										16	12	3	3	6				1						
1886	1	1								2		1	1	19	13	3	3	6					1	1				
1887	4		1	2	1					1		1		20	10		1	9										
1888										2		1	1	29	20		2	17			1		1					
1889										1			1	35	29	2	4	22										
1890	3			2	1					3	1	1	1	32	22	2	2	18					1	1	1			
1891	4			3	1					5		3	2	40	32	4	2	27							1			
1892	3		1	1			1							38	36		2	29			1	1						
1893	3						1	1		2		1	1	46	41	9	4	26				1	1			1		
1894	3			1			1	1		3		1	2	54		3	3	32				1	2					
1895	3				1		2			1			1	20	18		3	12					3					
Total	**50**	**6**	**6**	**21**	**7**	**1**	**5**	**2**	**2**	**31**	**3**	**18**	**10**	**750**	**428**	**67**	**74**	**252**	**1**	**1**	**3**	**9**	**18**	**3**	**13**	**3**	**1**	**1**

Year	Public Utilities							Halls, Houses & Cemetaries							Wholesale Trade						Retail Trade					
	430	431	432	433	435	436	439*	440	441	442	443	444	445	446	500	510	511*	512	520	530	600	610	611	620	630	690
1856	1		1																							
1857	6		5	1					1													3	1			
1858	8		5	3				1	1							1										
1859	3		3					1																		
1860	2		2					3		3																
1861	6		4	2				3	2			1				1					3	3	2			
1862	8		7		1			5	1		2	1	1								1	1	1			
1863	2		2					4	1		1					1					1	1				
1864	1		1					3		2	2			1		1					1	1				
1865	3		2			1		4	1			2		1	1	1					1	1				1
1866	4		2	2				5	2	1	1	2			2	2						1	1			
1867	3		3					4	1	1	1	1		1	2	1						1	1			
1868	5		4	1				3		1	1	2			2	1			1							
1869	5		4				1	2	1	1					1	1										
1870	4		3	1				4	1						3											
1871	5		5	1				9	6	1	1	1			3	1	1	1	2		1	1	1			
1872	3		3					7	5				1	1	4	2	2		1	1						
1873	2		2	1		1		8	3	2	1		1	2	2	2	1		1	1						
1874	4		3				1	9	5	1		1	1		2				1		2	2	2			
1875	5		4	1				3	2		1				3	1					1	1	1			
1876	3		1	2				10	6	2				2	2	2	1				1	1	1			1
1877	2		2					10	6	1	1		1	1	2	2		2								
1878	3				2		1	6	4					2	3	3	1	1			2	1				
1879	5		5					6	1						1	1			1	2						
1880	3		2	1				3	2	1				1	5	2	2	1	1		2	1				1
1881	3	2	1					6	5				1	1	2	2	3	2	1							
1882	2		2					8	7			1		1	2	1	1	4		1						
1883	4		3	1				3	2	1		1			4	3	1	1			2	1				1
1884	7		7					2	2						3	4				1						
1885	1							3	2	1					3	2										
1886	5		5					1	1						5	2				2	4	2				2
1887	5		4	1				5	2		1			2	5	3	2	1	1	2	1		1		2	
1888	6		4	2				3	1		2		3		8	2	1	1	1	5	1			1		
1889	4	1	3	1				2	2	3	1				2	1		1		1	1				1	
1890	3		2					6	1		1		1	1	6	5	3	3			3	2	1		1	1
1891	3		3					4	2				1	1	4	4	2	2		2	1					
1892								2	1		1		1		8	6	1	3		1	2	1	1			
1893	3		2					2			2		3		8	5	1	2	2		2	1				1
1894	5		3	2	1			8						1	8	7	1	5		1	2	1	1		1	
1895	2		1						2						2	2	2				2					2
Total	149	3	114	14	13	2	3	160	79	23	17	10	9	21	105	71	18	33	14	20	34	19	13	1	6	8

(continued)

Year	700	710	711	712	713	714	720	722*	730	740	800	810	820	830	831	832*	833*	840	841	842*	843*	850	860	861	870	871
	700	Domestic & Personal					Service				800			Mortgage				Investment							Finance, Insurance & Real Estate	
1856	1									1	1															
1857	1										1													1		
1858	1		1																							
1859	1	1	1						1																	
1860											1	1											1			
1861																										
1862	1	1								1	7	6														
1863	2	2								1	9	2		1	1										6	
1864	2	2		2						2	4		1												3	
1865	1	1								1	5														4	2
1866											2															
1867	2	2								2	1			1	1										1	
1868	2	2					1	1		1	3			1											1	
1869	2	2								2	2			1											5	
1870	2	2				1			1	1	5															
1871	2	2					1		3	1	6		1	2	2	1									3	
1872	5	5	1				1				9		3	4	4			1							2	1
1873	7	7							1	6	6		1	2		1		2	1		1				2	
1874	6	3	3							3	17		3	12	9	1		2	1	1						
1875	6								4	2	12		1	10	9	3									1	
1876	6	4	4						1	1	18			12	10	1	1	3	1	1						
1877	19	7	5			2	1		2	9	27			14	13	2	2	3	1	2					3	
1878	18	12	11	1			1			5	15			7	1	2	2	3		2					4	
1879	15	6	5	1					2	7	14		1	3	3			4		1	3		2	2	2	
1880	16	7	7						6	3	12			5	2		1	2		1	1				3	
1881	8	4	2	1	1				2	2	14	1	1	4	1						1				6	1
1882	8	1				1	2		4	1	24	6		5			2	2	2						11	
1883	14	4	2	2			1		4	5	14			4	1	2	1	2	1		1				6	
1884	13	6	2	3		1			2	5	12			5	1	1	1	3	2		1				3	
1885	7	2	1				1		5		13			5	4	1									8	
1886	10	1				1	2		1	6	15	1		4	1	3		5	4				1		6	
1887	12	2	2				1		5	4	16			7	4	1	2	3	2					1	4	
1888	13	2	2	1		1	1		10	2	21			6	4	1	1	3	2					1	7	
1889	14	5	4						7	5	15			4	2	1	1	4	4						2	1
1890	10	1		1			1		3	4	16	1		5	3		1	1	1			1	1		4	
1891	21	9	4	4	1				8	4	14			4	3				1	1		1			3	
1892	21	3	3	1			5		6	2	13			2	8	1		3	2						5	1
1893	15	7	6		1		3		3	7	20			8	8					1			3		5	1
1894	24	6	3	3			5		6	2	23			10	5	4	1	2	1	1					7	
1895	13	6	3	2		1	1		4	2	9			3	3		1	1	1	1	1				3	
Total	320	100	68	20	3	9	27	1	90	103	415	18	11	150	96	25	24	48	25	12	11	2	10	5	123	7

Year	Finance, Insurance & Real Estate						Agriculture, Forestry & Fishing													
	880 Real Estate			890 Others			900	910	Agriculture							920 Fishing				
	881	882*	883*	890	891*	892*			911	912*	913*	914*	915*	916*	917*		921	922	923
1856																			
1857							2									2		1	1
1858																			
1859																			
1860							1	1	1										
1861																			
1862	1						2	1		1						1			1
1863	1						3	3		2					1				
1864			1									2							
1865	1			1			6	4	1	1			1			2			2
1866				1	1		2	1	1							1			1
1867							1	1								1			1
1868				1			1	1		1									
1869	1						4	2	2							2		1	1
1870							1	1	1	1									
1871								2	1	1									
1872							3	2	2							1		1	
1873							3	3	1		1				1				1
1874							4	2	2							2		1	
1875																			1
1876	1			2		2	4	3	3	1						1			
1877	3						2	2				1							1
1878							1			1	1								
1879	1		1	2				3	1	1			1			1			
1880	1			1	1		3	3	1		1		1	1		1			1
1881			1	1			3	3					1	1					
1882							2	2		2		1	4		1	4			4
1883				2			12	8		2		2	1		1	2			2
1884							8	6		2	1	1	2		1	2			1
1885				1			9	9		2		1	4		2		1		
1886							5	3	1	1			1			2			
1887	2			1			3	3		2						2	2		
1888	2			1			3	3		3	1								
1889	3			3			3	2	2							1			1
1890	3			1			7	5	4							2			2
1891				4			3	3			1					3	1	1	
1892	2			2		1	6	4	2	1					1	2			2
1893	2			2			7	2	2							5	2		3
1894				4	1		4	3	1	2		1				1			1
1895	2						5	1	1	1						4			4
Total	15	1	2	29	3	2	133	91	26	27	6	7	15	2	8	42	6	4	31

(880 Total: 18; 900 Total shown above)

BIBLIOGRAPHY

ARCHIVAL SOURCES

<u>Scottish Record Office (West Register House)</u>

The Register of Defunct Companies (The file of each company is
given the prefix BT   2/   )

<u>Register of Companies, Edinburgh</u>

Files of active companies

<u>British Steel Corporation: Scottish Regional Record Centre, Glasgow</u>

Steel Company of Scotland, Ltd.,
Minute Books of the Board of Directors

<u>University of Aberdeen, Economic History Department</u>

The Northern Assurance Co. Ltd.,
Directors' Minute Books
Investment Ledgers

Scottish Metropolitan Assurance Co. Ltd.,
Directors' Minute Books

THESES

P.M. EDWARDS, "The Scottish Role in Midland America with Special Reference
to Wyoming, 1865-1895", Ph.D., University of St. Andrews, 1972

A. ESSEX-CROSBY, "Joint Stock Companies in Great Britain, 1890-1930",
M.Comm., University of London, 1937

N. GREISER, "The British Investor and his Sources of Information",
M.Sc.(Econ.), University of London, 1940

R.C. MICHIE, "The Scottish Stock Exchanges in the Nineteenth Century",
Ph.D., University of Aberdeen, 1979

BOOKS AND ARTICLES

J.D. BAILEY, "Australian Borrowing in Scotland in the Nineteenth Century",
<u>Economic History Review</u>, 2nd Series, XII (1959-60)

M. BLAIR, The Paisley Thread Industry (Paisley: Alexander Gardner, 1907)

BRITISH PARLIAMENTARY PAPERS, Select Committee on Limited Liability Acts, 1867, X

---- Select Committee on the Companies Acts, 1862 and 1867, 1877, VIII

A.F. BURNS AND W.C. MITCHELL, Measuring Business Cycles (New York: National Bureau of Economic Research, 1946)

J. BUTT, "The Scottish Oil Mania of 1864-6", Scottish Journal of Political Economy, XII (1965)

T.J. BYRES, "Entrepreneurship in the Scottish Heavy Industries, 1879-1900" in Payne (ed.), Studies in Scottish Business History

A.K. CAIRNCROSS, Home and Foreign Investment, 1870-1913 (Cambridge: Cambridge University Press, 1953)

R.H. CAMPBELL, "The Law and the Joint-Stock Company in Scotland" in P.L. Payne (ed.), Studies in Scottish Business History

S.G. CHECKLAND, The Mines of Tharsis (London: Allen & Unwin, 1967)

---- Scottish Banking: A History, 1695-1973 (Glasgow and London: Collins, 1975)

J. ROBERTSON CHRISTIE, "Joint Stock Enterprise in Scotland before the Companies Acts", The Juridicial Review, XXI (1909-10)

R.S. CRAIG, "Some Aspects of Capital Formation in Shipping in the Age of Sail and Steam", an unpublished paper delivered to the Ealing Business History Seminar, May 1975

I. DONNACHIE, A History of the Brewing Industry in Scotland (Edinburgh: John Donald, 1979)

A.B. DUBOIS, The English Business Company after the Bubble Act, 1720-1800 (New York: Octagon Books, 1971)

J. DUNNING, American Investment in British Manufacturing Industry (London: Allen & Unwin, 1958)

M. EDELSTEIN, "The Determinants of U.K. Investment Abroad, 1870-1913: the U.S. Case", Journal of Economic History, XXXIV (1974)

---- "Realised Rates of Return on U.K. Home and Overseas Portfolio Investment in the Age of High Imperialism", Explorations in Economic History, XIII (1976)

G. HEBERTON EVANS, JR., Business Incorporations in the United States, 1800-1943 (New York: National Bureau of Economic Research, 1948)

C.H. FEINSTEIN, National Income, Expenditure and Output of the United Kingdom, 1855-1965 (Cambridge: Cambridge University Press, 1972)

R.N. FORBES, "Some Contemporary Reactions to a Banking Failure", Three Banks Review, Number 121 (1979)

D.J.C. FORSYTH, U.S. Investment in Scotland (New York: Praeger, 1972)

I.F. GIBSON, "The Establishment of the Scottish Steel Industry", Scottish Journal of Political Economy, V (1958)

R. GIFFEN, The Growth of Capital (London: Bell, 1889)

F. GORE-BROWNE AND WILLIAM JORDAN, A Handy Book on the Formation, Management and Winding Up of Joint Stock Companies, 24th edition (London: Jordan & Sons, 1902)

R. GRAHAM, "The Investment Boom in British-Texan Cattle Companies, 1880-1885", Business History Review, XXXIV (1960)

H. HAMILTON, The Industrial Revolution in Scotland (Oxford: Oxford University Press, 1932)

L. HANNAH AND J.A. KAY, Concentration in Modern Industry (London: Macmillan, 1977)

P.E. HART AND S.J. PRAIS, "The Analysis of Business Concentration: A Statistical Approach", Journal of the Royal Statistical Society, Ser. A, 119 (1956)

P.E. HART, Studies in Profit, Business Saving and Investment in the United Kingdom, 1920-1962 (London: Allen & Unwin, 1965)

---- "On Bias and Concentration", Journal of Industrial Economics, XXVII (1978-79)

G.R. HAWKE AND M.C. REED, "Railway Capital in the United Kingdom in the Nineteenth Century", Economic History Review, XXII (1969)

W. TURRENTINE JACKSON, The Enterprising Scot: Investors in the American West after 1873 (Edinburgh: Edinburgh University Press, 1968)

J.B. JEFFERYS, "The Denomination and Character of Shares, 1855-1885", Economic History Review, XVI (1946)

---- Trends in Business Organisation in Great Britain since 1856 (New York: Arno Press, 1978)

W.P. KENNEDY, "Institutional Response to Economic Growth: Capital and Markets in Britain to 1914" in Les Hannah (ed.), Management Strategy and Business Development (London: Macmillan, 1976)

W.G. KERR, "Scottish Investment and Enterprise in Texas" in Payne (ed.), Studies in Scottish Business History

---- Scottish Capital and the American Credit Frontier (Austin, Texas: Texas State Historical Association, 1976)

F. LAVINGTON, The English Capital Market (London: Methuen, 1921)

W.R. LAWSON, The Scottish Investors' Manual: A Review of the Leading Scottish Securities in 1883 (Edinburgh and London: Blackwood & Sons, 1884)

C.H. LEE, The Quantitative Approach to Economic History (London: Martin Robertson, 1977)

L. LEVI, "On Joint Stock Companies", Journal of the Statistical Society, XXXIII (1870)

---- "The Progress of Joint Stock Companies with Limited and Unlimited Liability in the United Kingdom, during the Fifteen Years 1869-84", Journal of the Statistical Society, XLIX (1886)

H. LOWENFELD, All About Investment (London: Financial Review, 1909)

S.G.E. LYTHE AND J. BUTT, An Economic History of Scotland, 1100-1939 (Glasgow and London: Blackie, 1975)

D.H. MACGREGOR, "Joint Stock Companies and the Risk Factor", Economic Journal, XXXIX (1929)

---- Enterprise, Purpose and Profit (Oxford: Clarendon Press, 1934)

J. MACKENZIE, "Ship Owning by Shares and by Single Ship Companies", Accountants' Magazine, II (1898)

D.S. MACMILLAN, Scotland and Australia, 1788-1850 (Oxford: Oxford University Press, 1967)

---- "Scottish Enterprise in Australia, 1798-1879" in P.L. Payne (ed.), Studies in Scottish Business History

---- "The Transfer of Company Control from Scotland to London in the Nineteenth Century: The Case of the Scottish Australian Company, 1853", Business History, XII (1970)

A. MARSHALL, Industry and Trade (London: Macmillan, 1919)

---- Principles of Economics, 8th edition (London: Macmillan, 1920)

W.H. MARWICK, "The Limited Company in Scottish Economic Development", Economic History, IV (1937)

B.R. MITCHELL, Abstract of British Historical Statistics (Cambridge: Cambridge University Press, 1962)

F.W. PAISH, "The London New Issue Market", Economica, New Series, XVIII (1951)

P.L. PAYNE, Rubber and Railways in the Nineteenth Century (Liverpool: Liverpool University Press, 1961)

---- (ed.), Studies in Scottish Business History (London: Cass, 1967)

---- "The Savings Bank of Glasgow, 1836-1914" in P.L. Payne (ed.), Studies in Scottish Business History

---- "Industrial Entrepreneurship and Management in Great Britain" in P. Mathias and M.M. Postan (eds.), The Cambridge Economic History of Europe, VII, The Industrial Economies: Capital, Labour and Enterprise (Cambridge: Cambridge University Press, 1978)

---- Colvilles and the Scottish Steel Industry (Oxford: Clarendon Press, 1979)

S.J. PRAIS, The Evolution of Giant Firms in Britain (Cambridge: Cambridge University Press, 1976)

J. PROSSER, "The Incorporation of Trading Companies", Accountants' Magazine, II (1898)

W.D. RUBINSTEIN, "The Victorian Middle Classes: Wealth, Occupation, and Geography", Economic History Review, 2nd Series, XXX (1977)

J. SCOTT AND M. HUGHES, "Ownership and Control in a Satellite Economy: A Discussion from Scottish Data", Sociology, X (1976)

J. SCOTT, M. HUGHES AND J. MACKENZIE, "Patterns of Ownership in Top Scottish Companies", Scottish Journal of Sociology, I (1976)

J. SCOTT AND M. HUGHES, The Anatomy of Scottish Capital (London: Croom Helm, 1980)

H.A. SHANNON, "The Coming of General Limited Liability", Economic History, II (1931)

---- "The First Five Thousand Limited Companies and their Duration", Economic History, II (1932)

---- "The Limited Companies of 1866-83", Economic History Review, IV (1932-33)

D.K. SHEPPARD, The Growth and Role of U.K. Financial Institutions, 1880-1962 (London: Methuen, 1971)

A. SLAVEN, "Earnings and Productivity in the Scottish Coal-Mining Industry during the Nineteenth Century: The Dixon Enterprises" in Payne (ed.), Studies in Scottish Business History

C.C. SPENCE, <u>British Investment and the American Mining Frontier</u>, (Ithaca, New York: Cornell University Press, 1958)

W.A. THOMAS, <u>The Provincial Stock Exchanges</u> (London: Cass, 1973)

G. TODD, "Some Aspects of Joint Stock Companies, 1844-1900", <u>Economic History Review</u>, IV (1932-33)

UNITED STATES CENTRAL STATISTICAL BOARD, <u>Standard Industrial Classification</u> (Washington, D.C., 1939-40)

L. WEATHERILL, <u>One Hundred Years of Paper-Making: An Illustrated History of the Guardbridge Paper Company Ltd., 1873-1973</u> (Guardbridge, Fife: Guardbridge Paper Co. Ltd., 1974)

M. WILKINS, <u>The Emergence of Multinational Enterprise: American Business Abroad from the Colonial Era to 1914</u> (Cambridge, Mass.: Harvard University Press, 1970)

W. WOODRUFF, "The American Origins of a Scottish Industry", <u>Scottish Journal of Political Economy</u>, II (1955)

---- <u>The Rise of the British Rubber Industry during the Nineteenth Century</u> (Liverpool: Liverpool University Press, 1958)

INDEX

Clothing, 63, 66.

Clyde Jute Works, 104n.

Clydesdale Bank, 56, 75n.

Coats, Archibald, 64, 65, 73, 82.

Coats, J. and P., 65.

Coats, Sir James, 17n.

Coats, Peter, 17n.

Coats, Thomas, 73.

Coffee plantations, 62.

Coffee shops, 60.

Colliery companies, 10, 56-8, 80.

Colorado Land and Mortgage Co., 52.

Co-operatives, 51.

Colt, Samuel, 55n.

Commercial Bank of Scotland, 75n.

Common informer, 6n.

Companies Office, Edinburgh, 2n, 5.

Company promoters, 9, 10, 22, 30, 48.

Computer, use of, in analyzing company data, 203, 17.

Concentration, industrial, 96.

Consolidated Copper Co. of Canada, 62.

Conversions of partnerships into limited companies, 57-9, 65, 66, 67, 69, 82, 89, 93.

Copper mining, 56.

Cornwall, 11.

Cotton-thread, 65.

Cottrell, P.L., 1n, 46n, 51n.

Craig, R.S., 67n.

Cunninghame, Alexander, 58, 90.

Davie, William, 66n.

Debentures, 48, 90, 91.

Deer Trail Land and Cattle Co., 64.

Denny, Peter, 66n.

Denny, William, and Brothers, 66n.

Directors, 17, 23, 45, 73.

Dissolution of companies, 24-7; modes of, 8.

Distillery companies, 10, 59-60.

Dividends, 105n, 106n.

Dixon, William, 57.

Dixon, William, and Co., 57.

Dixon, William, Ltd., 58.

Dixon, William Smith, 57, 58n.

Dixon's Ironworks, 57.

Donnachie, Ian, 14n, 65n.

Drapery companies, 100n.

DuBois, A.B., 30n.

Dundee, 26, 48, 52, 63, 64.

Dundee Aerated Water Manufacturing Co., 59.

Dunning, John, 55n.

East Bengal Co., 62n.

Economist, The, 105n.

Edelstein, Michael, 81n, 89n, 105-6.

Edinburgh, 2, 26, 48, 52, 63, 64.

Edinburgh Courant, 48n.

Edinburgh Gazette, 6.

Edinburgh Heritable Securities Co., 60n.

Edwards, P.M., 49n.

Eglinton Chemical Co., 59.

Electrical machinery, 66.

Electricity companies, 100, 101.

Engineering companies, 63, 65, 66, 101, 107.

Entrepreneurial expectations, 23.

Entrepreneurship, 100.

Essex-Crosby, A., 14n, 42n, 46n, 73n, 94n.

Evans, G. Heberton, 1, 11n, 22, 97n.

Ewing, Archibald Orr, 59.

Falkirk Joint Stock Gas Co., 53n.

Feinstein, C.H. 95n.

Ferguson, John, 71.

Fife Coal Co., 57.

Finance and Insurance companies, 10, 80, 92-3, 102-3.

Financial press, 81.

Findlay, Thomas Dunlop, 66n.

Finlaw, Maj. J., 71.

Fitz-Wygram, Loftus, 14n.

Fleming, James Nicol, 66n.

Fleming, Robert, 63, 64.

Flemington Coal Co., 57.

Food companies, 63, 65, 101, 107.

Forbes, R.N., 61n.

Forsyth, D.J.C., 55n.
Fraud, 10, 30, 31, 45, 48n, 108.
Freight charges, 107.

Galbraith, James, 66n.
Garpel Hematite Co., 5n.
Gartcraig Coal and Fireclay Co., 57.
Gas companies, 36n, 53, 92, 100, 101.
Gibrat's Law, 104.
Gibson, I.F., 59n.
Giffen, R., 45, 93.
Glasgow, 26, 48, 64.
Glasgow and South-Western Railway, 51, 52.
Glasgow and West of Scotland Newspaper Co., 59.
Glasgow Bessemer Steel Co., 59.
Glasgow Heritable Securities Co., 60n.
Glasgow Port Washington Iron and Coal Co., 61.
Glass products, 63.
Glengarnock Iron Co., 58.
Gold-mining, 82.
Goodyear, Charles, 55.
Gore-Browne, F., and William Jordan, 5n, 6n, 9, 14n, 17n, 24n.
Goven Forge Co., 58-9.
Graham, Richard, 64.
Greenock, 64.
Greenock Steamship Co., 66.
Greiser, N., 81n.
Guard Bridge Paper Co., 59.

Haig, The, family, 59.
Hallside, 91.
Hamilton, Henry, 58n.
Hannah, L., 49n.
Hannah, L., and J.A. Kay, 96-7.
Hansford Land and Cattle Co., 64.
Harris, Fred W., and James Dixon, 71.
Hart, P.E., 97n, 104n.
Hart, P.E., and S.J. Prais, 96.
Harveyhill Copper Co., 62.
Hawke, G.R., and M.C. Reed, 79n.
Henderson, J. and P., and Co., 72.

Henderson, Robert, 66n.

Heritable Property Trust, 60n.

Highland Mexican Land and Live Stock Co., 64.

Holding companies, 93.

Huntington Copper and Sulphur Co., 62.

Huntington, Lucius S., 62.

Hydropathic establishments, 60.

India, Scottish investment in, 62.

Insurance companies, 93n.

Interlocking interests, 73.

Investors, see also Shareholders, 30, 45, 49n, 51, 52, 53, 81-3, 104, 106.

Investment, consequences of, 107; Scottish, overseas, 1, 12, 61-4.

Investment Trusts, 62-4.

Inverness, 62, 64.

Ireland, D.S., 14n.

Irrawady Flotilla Co., 66.

Iron and Steel companies, 56-8, 65, 80, 91, 101, 107.

Irvine, 59.

Jackson, W. Turrentine, 1, 11, 61n, 63n, 64n.

Jefferys, J.B., 1n, 13n, 14n, 46n, 57, 58, 65, 67, 73n, 75n, 79, 83, 95n, 108.

Joint Stock Companies Acts, 2, 5, 6, 8, 14, 53, 56, 80, 83.

Joint Stock Companies, average length of life of, by industrial classification,
      101; capital of, 12-16, 74-81; capital formation by Scottish, 89-94,
      and British, 94-5; demography of the early Scottish, 13-53;
      determination of dates of birth and death of Scottish, 5-7; English,
      34, 36-9, 42, 44, 45-6; factors affecting length of life of, 97-100;
      life expectancy of, 31, 34-45, 53, 96; methods used in classifying,
      8-12; nature of data contained in files relating to Scottish, 4;
      number incorporated, 18-22, 54, in existence, 31-33, dissolved, 21-7,
      and sold, amalgamated or reconstructed, 25-6, 42-3, 86, 99; ownership
      and control of, 16-8, 26; questions asked of data relating to, in
      Scotland, 3; Scottish, compared with English, 77, 79, 108-9; share
      denominations of, 50-1; size of, and rate of growth, 97, 102-4;
      records of, in London, 1, and Scotland, 1-2.

Jute, 62.

Kennedy, W.P., 17n, 49n, 100n, 105n.

Kerr, W.G., 1, 11, 63n.

King, Sir James, of Campsie, 73.

Land and Cattle companies, 10, 11, 14, 61, 63-4, 80, 80n; see also Ranching
   craze.
Lavington, F., 90n, 94n, 95.
Law of Proportionate Effect, see Gibrat's Law.
Lawson, W.R., 48, 64.
Lead mining, 56.
Lee, C.H., 13n.
Levi, Leone, 12, 29n, 34.
Life expectancy, factors affecting, of companies, 97-100; see also Joint
   Stock Companies.
Limited Liability Joint Stock Company List, 13n.
Limitation of Liability, 46.
Liquidation, of companies, 5, 24, 83, 84-5; see also Joint Stock Companies.
Liquidator, 5.
Little, James, and Co., 69.
Liverpool, 49n, 67.
Local connections, importance of, in attracting funds, 52.
Local recruitment of capital, 79n.
Lochore and Capledrae Cannel Coal Co., 57.
London, 26, 29, 48.
Lowenfeld, Henry, 100n.
Lythe, S.G.E., and John Butt, 81n.

M'Ausland, John, 66n.
McCloskey, D.N., 49n.
McEwan, William, 65.
MacGregor, D.H., 5n, 6n, 12, 22, 29, 36n, 77n, 89n, 109n.
Mackenzie, James, 67n.
Mackie and Thomson, 70.
McKinnell, H., 57.
McLagan, Peter, of Pumpherston, 73.
Maclay and M'Intyre, 69-72.
Macmillan, D.S., 26n, 49n, 61n.
McMurray, James, 70-2.
Manchester, 49n.
Manufacturing companies, 80-1, 95; average length of life of, 101; and
   capital formation, 89-92; growth of, 102-4; Scottish investment
   in, 55-6, 65-6.
Mapleton Farming Co., 64.
Marshall, Alfred, 22, 23, 96n.

Oregon and Washington Trust Investment Co., 63.
Overseas investment, Scottish, 1, 12, 61-4; amount of, 81.

Paisley, 65.
Paish, F.W., 95.
Paper companies, 101.
Park Red River Valley Land Co., 64.
Patara Silver Lead Mining and Smelting Co., 61.
Patents, exploitation of, 52, 55, 66, 91.
Payne, P.L., 23n, 30n, 52n, 56n, 59n, 73n, 82n, 104n.
Peru, Scottish investment in, 61.
Photographic equipment, 66.
Potteries, 56.
Prairie Cattle Co., 16, 63.
Prais, S.J., 97n.
Private companies, 79, 105.
Probate records, 17n.
Prosser, John, 9n, 17n.
Public amenities, 107.
Public Halls, 51, 107.
Public Utility companies, 39, 53, 56, 80, 92, 95; growth of, 102-3;
        length of life of, 100-1.

Railway carriage and wagon builders, 56.
Railway companies, 79, 100n.
Ranching craze, 14n, 63.
Rawyards Coal Co., 57.
Real Estate companies, 92-3, 100-1; Scottish investment in American, 62-3.
Register of Joint Stock Companies, 5, 6, 86.
Registrar of Joint Stock Companies, 4n, 5, 6, 7, 15, 34n, 46, 62, 77.
Redi, Thomas, 73.
Retail trade, 101, 102-3.
Return, on equity capital, 106.
Rio Tinto, 61.
Robb, Moore and Co., 71.
Rowan, John M., 59.
Rubber, 55.
Rubinstein, W.D., 17n.

Savings Bank of Glasgow, 48, 60n.

Scientific instruments, 66.

Scotland, American enterprise in, 55; commercial morality in, 30; experience
of joint stock companies in, a regional example, 108; the law
and the joint stock company in, 30; savings generated in, 82;
standard of living in, 107.

Scott, John, and Michael Hughes, 74n.

Scottish American Investment Company, 51, 63.

Scottish American Investment Trust, 52, 63.

Scottish Heritages Co., 60n.

Scottish Indian Coffee Co., 62.

Scottish Provident Investment Co., 60n.

Select Committee on the Companies Act of 1862-1867, 4n, 77.

Service trades, 102-3.

Shannon, H.A., 1, 6, 7n, 8, 11n, 12, 29, 30n, 34, 36, 39, 51, 67n, 96, 104n,
105n, 108.

Share denominations, 13-6, 49-51, 69.

Shares, forfeit of, 24.

Shareholders, 15, 17, 24, 48, 69-73, 75, 79n, 82-3, 95, 98, 100, 108;
calculation of loss by, 86-7; estimated true loss by, 88-9; return to,

Sheppard, D.K., 93n.

Ship brokers, 69-72.

Shipbuilding companies, 58-9, 65, 107.

Shipping companies, 10-11, 53, 66-72, 80, 84n, 100n, 107; see also Single-ship
companies.

Simpson, George, 57.

Single-ship companies, 67-72, 80, 92.

Slaven, A., 58n.

Sloan, James R., 70.

Social Clubs, 51.

Social Science Research Council, 2.

Sokolowski, Helena, 2.

Somerset House, 1.

Smith, John Guthrie, 64.

Smith, W. Macadam, 70-2.

Spain, Scottish investment in, 61.

Spence, Clark C., 83n.

Standard Industrial Classification, 11.

State Line Steamship Co., 66.

State Steamship Co., 66n.

Steel Company of Scotland, 59, 91.

Stephen, Alex, and Co., 70-2.

Stephen, John, 70-2.

Stevenson, James, 70, 72.

Stone products, 63.

Stewart, A. and J., 104n.

Stewart, A. and J., and Clydesdale Ltd., 104n.

Stewart, A. and J., and Menzies, 104n.

Stewarts and Lloyds, 104n.

"Summary of Capital and Shares", 4, 7.

Tea shops, 60.

Telegraph companies, 100n.

Telephone companies, 100n.

Temperance movement, 60.

Tennant, Sir Charles, 17n, 73, 83n, 91.

Texas Land and Cattle Co., 63.

Texas Land and Mortgage Co., 52.

Textile companies, 100, 101.

Tharsis Sulphur and Copper Co., 61.

Thomas, W.A., 95.

Thomson, Dickie, and Co., 69.

Tod and McGregor, 58.

Todd, Geoffrey, 1n, 12, 29n, 31n, 34n, 36n, 45.

Trade Clyde, 53, 96, 100; and company formation, 18-22, 77; and company
        dissolutions, 22-26; and companies sold, amalgamated or reconstructed,
        26; influence of, on timing of promotional and incorporational
        activity, 108-9.

Tyson, R.E., 61n, 75n.

Umpherston and Co., 59.

Unincorporated companies in Scotland, 30.

Union Bank of Scotland, 56, 75.

United Alkali, 59.

Universal Mining and Exploration Co., 11.

Urquhart, David Ingles, 57.

Warrender, Sir George, 64.

Water companies, 36n, 53, 92, 100, 101.

Weatherill, Lorna, 59n.

Weir, William, 17n.
West of Scotland Lands and Buildings Investment Co., 60n.
West Register House, Edinburgh, 2, 48.
Western American Cattle Co., 64.
Western American Land Co., 64.
Wholesale trade, 102-3.
Wilkins, Mira, 55n.
Willis, George, 57.
Wills, 17n.
Wilson, W., 70.
Winding-up, **see also** Liquidation, 4, 5, 24.
Wood products, 63.
Woodruff, J., 55n.
Wright and Breakenridge, 69.
Writing down, of capital, 14, 16, 84n.
Wyoming Cattle Ranch Co., 63.

Yeats, Andrew, and Co., 57.
Young, James "Paraffin", 55.
Younger, William, 65.